The *Percy Bass* Book of

TRADITIONAL DECORATION

By Jennie Elias

With photographs by Philip Cayford and foreword by Jane Morris

for Charlie & India Clegg

Copyright
Text: © 2005 Jennie Elias
Photographs: © 2005 Philip Cayford

Art Direction by Henrik Williams.

Designed by Roberto Filistad.

Additional layout by
Joanna Bettles and Sarah Jane Muskett.

Edited by Caroline Blake and Caroline Harrison.

Production by Dave Stanford.

Published by

SPG MEDIA LIMITED

Printed in China

ISBN 1 85938 538 9

CONTENTS

FOREWORD

I started running Percy Bass over 20 years ago, and these have been some of the most rewarding and enjoyable years of my life.

Recently, the world of interior decorating has seen an increased emphasis on styling, often at the expense of quality and longevity. But for the discerning customer, these three features go hand in hand. At Percy Bass, I have endeavoured to maintain high standards of traditional skills, especially in the manufacture of upholstery and curtains. Whilst we have adapted our style to incorporate contemporary fashions, we have kept high-quality workmanship as a key priority.

The Percy Bass interior design team has decorated houses around the world, and we have thoroughly enjoyed working with customers of every nationality.

This is our first decorating book, so we have included some of the suppliers who have supported us over the years and excel in their fields.

We have always been so busy that, until now, we have never photographed or documented our work. I hope this book will give you a taste of the precision, skill and care that we employ when decorating a client's house to the highest possible standard.

Jane Morris

Jane Morris

Left: This small dining room has a formal, yet cosy, atmosphere: Berkeley sprig wallpaper with a Colefax & Fowler blind is teamed with cream coloured cotton damask curtains by Ian Sanderson, trimmed with red bullion fringe and tie backs by Ramm Son & Crocker.

The rear of Percy Bass in Crescent Place, virtually unchanged in nearly 100 years.

NO PERMANENT PARKING OF VEHICLES

L. RICH

INTRODUCTION

P ercy Bass is an interior decorating emporium located in one of London's most fashionable streets – Chelsea's Walton Street. Starting as an upholstery and curtain-making business, Percy Bass has been at this location for nearly 100 years.

Over the years, the development of Percy Bass has been largely influenced by the forces of social, economic and stylistic change. These influences have also been reflected in the style and character of Walton Street, the location with which Percy Bass is synonymous.

It is interesting to observe that the appearance of the street has changed very little during the last century, but its community, traders and amenities have altered considerably. Walton Street has now become a destination for the fashion conscious, whether they be shopping for their home, their children, or for themselves; but it was not always so.

In Victorian times, as commercial activity developed in West London, the Walton Street area became a centre for services and suppliers to cater to the residents of the newly built homes in Knightsbridge and Chelsea. The street was a bustling place, with two dairies, a butchers, a bakers, a grocers, an undertaker, a haberdashers, a watchmaker and coffee rooms. Walton Street would have been incredibly noisy, with the constant clatter of horses' hooves passing by. There was also a police station, which is now a traffic warden headquarters.

Top right: The Percy Bass shop in 2002.

Above right: Jane Morris and Jenny Bond outside Percy Bass in the late 1970s before the purchase of 184 and 186 Walton St.

Above left: The Percy Bass Shop as it is today.

W.D. Hodges & Co., the predecessor of Percy Bass, was the first factory in Walton Street, and its employees would have been regular users of the street's facilities.

THE ORIGINS OF WALTON STREET
The street, originally known as June Street, takes its name from George Walton Onslow. He was a trustee of the Smith's Charity Estate that owned part of the land on the northeast of the street. Originally, the site was a 14-acre field, known as the Quail Field, and was used as grazing pasture prior to becoming a successful market garden. In 1840, part of the area became a cricket ground called Prince's Club. The grounds included a skating rink that a woman would not be admitted unless she had first been presented at Court, even if her husband was a member.

The first part of the street to be laid out on the Prince's Club grounds was Walton Place, at the extreme-north end of the site. One of the first buildings in the street was St. Saviour's Church, and soon after its construction, twin terraces of nine stucco-fronted houses were developed nearby. These terraces remain almost exactly as they were when completed in 1844, and are located adjacent to Harrods. The rest of Walton Street, with its terraced houses and shops, was laid out in 1847. These

In the late 1890s, there were still many market gardens in the Walton Street area, with a small river close by

and were located on the southeastern side of Walton Street. The area is now Lennox Gardens, Lennox Garden Mews, Clabon Mews and part of Cadogan Square. The southern boundary of the club was The Australian public house in Milner Terrace (now Milner Street), possibly named to commemorate the Australian cricket team's first international match in England. The fashionable Prince's Club was so exclusive

stucco-fronted houses, with modest architectural embellishments, were in marked contrast to the buildings in adjoining Pont Street. These were predominately red-brick mansion houses in the high-Victorian Queen Anne style, and were built on the remainder of the Prince's Club site in the 1870s and 1880s. Their grandiose, elaborate style is now known as 'Pont Street Dutch'.

Right: Walton Street and Walton Place, c.1910.

In 1882, the architect Richard Norman Shaw designed Walton House, on Walton Street, for Mr Edward Kennedy. This building still survives, and is now converted to flats. Another former resident of Walton Street is the author P.G. Wodehouse, who lived at number 16 from 1918 to 1920. He situated his formidable fictional character, Aunt Agatha, in nearby Pont Street.

THE ORIGINS OF THE SHOP

At the turn of the nineteenth century, the current Percy Bass shop at 184 Walton Street was a dwelling house. But the property known today as the Percy Bass building was actually at 188 Walton Street and linked with the building behind, 13 Crescent Place. These buildings were owned by a family from the Welsh borders called Hodges. At the time, the rear of the premises in Crescent Place was used to house carriages, with stables for the horses and storage for hay. In 1895, William David Hodges founded his painting and decorating business in these premises and named the company, and the shop in Walton Street, W.D. Hodges & Co. The company was highly regarded and worked on prestigious projects such as Apsley House, the magnificent Hyde Park Corner house of the Duke of Wellington, known as Number 1 London. In the late 1890s, there were still many market gardens in the Walton Street area, with a small river and bridge close by.

Percy Bass himself came to Walton Street in the 1920s, and rented workshop space from the Hodges family in order to set up his upholstery business. The company Percy Bass Ltd. was set up as a new business in 1930, and by this time it was specialising in fine-quality upholstery and curtain-making. Along with Percy Bass, Sid Stoneman was an original director of Percy Bass Ltd. and a minority shareholder. He was the company's principal pattern cutter and estimator, and spent almost his entire life working there.

Throughout the 1930s, Percy Bass prospered. However, the advent of the Second World War in 1939 saw the company turn its skills to producing blackout curtains (to protect against the Luftwaffe bombing raids). By this time, the Hodges family no longer operated their painting business, but remained the

Above left: Walton Street at the corner of Draycott Avenue looking east, c.1905. Percy Bass is in the left foreground, after the gabled building.

Above: The police station, Walton Street, c.1910.

landlords of the building. During the war years, a blacksmith continued to operate from the rear of the Percy Bass premises and Louis Rich, an antique restorer and furniture decorator, moved into the ground floor of the building. Louis Rich's business complemented Percy Bass, and the two companies mutually benefited from being in the same building. The two businesses continue to cooperate to this day.

Walton Street survived the wartime bombing, and in the mid-1960s further development took place when the Cadogan Estate built a terrace of 36 sympathetically styled houses on the north side of the street. Following the war, Percy Bass reverted to its traditional business of high-quality upholstery and curtain making, and occupied the entire Walton Street and Crescent Place site (except for the part,

porcelain breakages for wealthy customers, including royalty, and interior decorating shops Plus 2 and Churnifur also took up residence on the street. Ruth Bellord opened a shop to make and sell tables in any shape or style, whilst Susan Llewellyn sold small and pretty antique pieces, trinkets, pill boxes and jewellery. Charles Bereford-Clark (formerly of Colefax & Fowler) had an antique shop next to Hawkes the jewellers and the Justin de Blanc Hygienic Bakery.

On the south side of the street, at number 13, was Raymond Le Brun, specialising in quality oriental antiques. Keal & Douglas opened at number 19. This business was run by Bobby Keal, known for his magnificent eye for colour. Keal & Douglas had thousands of curtain pattern books and carpets to choose

Opposite: An innovative scheme for a shoe showroom, with roman blinds by Sahco Hesslein, window seat covered in GP & J Baker and cushions by de la Cuona.

Percy Bass prides itself on accommodating any request, no matter how unusual

sublet to Louis Rich). At the time, Mrs Dean ran the curtain workshop on the first floor and oversaw the rows of seamstresses who worked there. Sadly, Percy Bass died in April 1969, so his son Eric Bass took over the company with Sid Stoneman and ran it in very much the same style as his father.

Following the establishment of Percy Bass, a shop called Home Decorating opened in 1954 at 83 Walton Street. This business was run by two sisters, Lady Garnett and Lilah Fortescue. They sold wallpapers from France, as well as a huge range of papers and materials that could not be obtained anywhere else in the country. They also stocked wallpapers from Cole & Son, and ran a do-it-yourself service by hiring out equipment such as papering tables and ladders. Even The Queen visited the shop to place some special orders.

A HIVE OF INDUSTRY
By the 1970s, Walton Street, though still a mixture of shops and private houses, began to establish itself as an area for the discerning, fashion-conscious homemaker to visit. Chinamend repaired valuable

from, as well as specialist, painted furniture, gilding and decorative antiques. Customers included Kelpie Buchanan, who ran George Spencer, the decorating shop in Sloane Street. This eccentric character would arrive by scooter, wearing a cloak. Next door, at number 17, was The Walton Street Stationery Company, a stylish black and white shop designed by David Hicks. At number 21 was The Express Dairy and Perrins was at number 23. Perrins was an antique shop and general restorer, with a workshop at the back. Other home-decorating-based shops in the area were Mary John Antiques, Dudley Poplak (with clients including the Prince and Princess of Wales) and Michael Szell, dealing in exclusive fabrics.

Walton Street's restaurants included La Popote, Jacaranda, San Martino and Walton's, which was damaged by an IRA bomb in the 1970s. Ma Cuisine at number 113 was awarded a Michelin star in 1975. One of the last amenity shops in the area was Ferguson's, situated next to Home Decorating. This grocer sold fresh coffee,

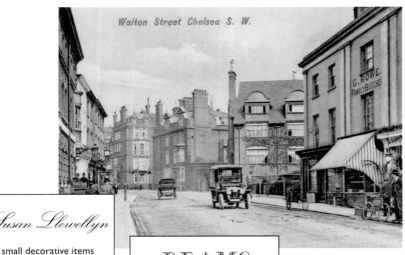

Walton Street Chelsea S. W.

Top: Walton Street, with Ovington Street to the right, c.1910. The buildings on the left have since been demolished and rebuilt.

Above, right and below: Advertisements from the early 1970's for some of Walton Street's decorative shops, which have all since disappeared.

which was ground to order, and biscuits that were weighed out into paper bags. The mahogany counter always had a whole, ripe Brie on display.

Percy Bass continued to be the principal manufacturer of upholstered furniture and custom-made curtains on Walton Street, and grew rapidly as it served the growing West London decorating profession. The company became an important supplier to the decorating trade and when Eric Bass (the last member of the Bass family) died in 1976, the business was taken over by one of its main customers – the talented and famous international interior decorator, Algernon Asprey. Algernon had previously relied on the skills, quality and precision of the Percy Bass workshop for the execution of his decorating contracts, so he bought the company to secure its future and the continuity of his supply.

It was under Algernon's ownership that Percy Bass first opened the retail and decorating side of its business to augment the production of upholstery and curtains for the decorating trade. Jane Morris joined Percy Bass in 1979 and opened 188 Walton Street (which had hitherto been used as the entrance to the workshops) as an interior design shop.

In 1985, Jane Morris became the owner of Percy Bass. Since then, she has developed the business into one of the UK's best-known decorating houses, whilst continuing to supply traditionally made, high-quality upholstery and curtains to other designers, as well as to Percy Bass's own customers. Percy Bass remains the longest standing business resident in Walton Street.

MODERN TIMES

Today, the smart shops on Walton Street serve the local community, visitors from around London, day shoppers from the country and tourists from all over the world. It is hardly surprising that this street is so popular, as there are a dozen designer fashion shops, eight restaurants and bars, six art galleries, eight jewellers, as well as speciality food and wine shops. There are also 12 irresistible shops offering products for the home. These products include exclusive bed linens, needlepoint cushions, oriental carpets, light fittings and lamps, customised stationery, wedding list gifts, ceramic tiles and Meissen porcelain. In addition to these homeware shops, Walton Street is now home to nine interior decorating outlets – two specialising solely in childrens' rooms. If you add the street's geographical position to these attractions – close to Harrods in Knightsbridge, as well as the designer shops and famous restaurants of Beauchamp Place and Brompton Cross in Chelsea, the result is shopping paradise!

Simply taking a stroll along this street is a delight. The Royal Borough Council has installed black wrought-iron Victorian-style lamp posts that are in keeping with the village atmosphere. In summer, these are draped in magenta and white petunia baskets that form a seaonal line of colour

waste paper baskets fill the shop, and often look as if they are about to topple over. There is an eclectic assortment of decorative items to choose from, or order, in any design or colour. Dogs predominate. Any breed's image can become a note pad, cachepot, tray, waste paper basket, bookend or cushion.

Percy Bass is a quirky shop that prides itself on accommodating any request that a customer might have. This can range from creating a sofa based on a picture torn from a magazine, to supplying fringe or braid to match an antique or favourite fabric. Some requests are more eccentric, but are accepted nevertheless.

Although many key support industries to the decorating trade have struggled to survive in a world where young people are reluctant to take on a five-year apprenticeship, and children have no wish to enter the family business, Percy Bass remains optimistic.

There is an eclectic assortment of decorative items to choose from, in any design or colour

and joy. Chelsea is, after all, the location of the world-renowned Chelsea Flower Show. In winter, the lamp posts become mini Christmas trees, bedecked with electric fairy lights that sparkle as dusk falls.

To the west of the street, near the junction with Draycott Avenue, the Percy Bass shop is nearly hidden by its green and white striped awning. You could almost miss this discreet shop as you walk along Walton Street, were it not for the piles of goodies stacked in the window to catch your eye. If you suddenly need an urgent birthday present for a friend, a fun 'message' cushion for a loved one, novelty bookends, an original hand-painted lavatory seat or stocking fillers, this is the ideal gift shop. Many items are inexpensive. Trays and

There will always be a segment of the market where style is more important than quality, but Percy Bass is confident that the work that goes into top-quality traditional decorating will always be appreciated by discerning clients. Quality craftsmanship will always be in demand, and will continue to be applied to Percy Bass's products and projects, no matter what fashion dictates.

Much of the company's interior design work is for the export market. Despite the fickleness of style, Percy Bass has managed to adapt and survive without compromising its principles on traditional quality, and it will undoubtedly continue to do so in the future. In the midst of a quick-fix generation, the preservation of traditional crafts at Percy Bass is a veritable treasure. **PB**

Clockwise from right:
Watercolours that Algernon Asprey produced during his schooldays indicate his budding artistic talent.

Black seal leather box with silver-gilt embellishments incorporating the signs of the Zodiac

Marbled leather box with the initials of the bride and groom.

Clockwise from right:

Crystal egg, containing phial of scent.

British Luxury Fair, Dubai 1976.

Gun cabinets to house rifles for Holland & Holland, the premier English gun maker.

Gold and jewelled pendant brooches.

Algernon Asprey was part of the sixth generation of the family goldsmith, silversmith and jewellery emporium Asprey & Co. of Bond Street, London's most exclusive shopping street. This company was initially established in 1781 by Algernon's ancestor, William Asprey. Asprey & Co. is a royal warrant holder; every monarch since Queen Victoria has patronised Asprey's.

Born in 1912, Algy (as he was known) attended Charterhouse School. The watercolours that he produced during his schooldays indicate his budding artistic talent. He then studied at the Regent Street Polytechnic Art School, before taking a commission in the Royal Scots Guards during the Second World War. Having established himself as an accomplished goldsmith and silversmith at the family firm, Algy later branched out into furniture design and, following a family dispute in 1971, started his own interior design business at 27 Bruton Street.

Prior to purchasing Percy Bass in 1976, Algy had been employing the company to supply the upholstery and curtain-making requirements of his interior design and decorating contracts. His extensive list of clients included most of the royal families of the world, as well as the owners of large landmark houses in England. When

ALGERNON ASPREY

executing his commissions, Algernon's practice was to subcontract specialist work to small, reliable, high-quality workshops; thus Percy Bass became one of his main suppliers. This approach worked well, and Algy gained a reputation for delivering projects on time and on budget, due to his hard work and acute attention to detail.

BY ROYAL APPOINTMENT

By the time he took over Percy Bass in 1976, Algy had been commissioned to design no fewer than seven royal palaces, including Al Nassiria, the largest palace in Saudi Arabia. These orders brought huge benefits to British craftsmen, and provided clients with enormous pleasure. As well as owning Percy Bass, Algy also owned a company called Elmounts that specialised in making silver items and leather wallets for Asprey's. This company was also housed in the Percy Bass building at 13 Crescent Place. These small companies prided themselves on their excellence, and were one of the reasons why Algy was able to satisfy his clients' exacting demands, ensuring that his reputation soared.

During the 1980s, there was a growth in the demand for quality design. Other well-known interior designers, such as David Mlinaric, John Siddeley (Lord Kenilworth) and Mann & Fleming were attracted to Percy Bass for the production of quality upholstery and curtains. At this time, the top floor of the Percy Bass building was used entirely for curtain-making, while the first floor was dedicated to upholstery.

In addition to his interior decorating business, Algy always responded to requests for individually designed objects and trophies, and he completed commissions for the royal families of the UK, Nepal, Luxembourg, Greece and Jordan. He also designed gun cabinets to house rifles for Holland & Holland, the premier English gun maker.

In 1979, with family disagreements behind him, Algy transferred his decorating business to Asprey's. By this time, Algy was 67 years old. In 1982, the family company was restructured and it was decided that the decorating department would not be part of the future of the business. The department in Bond Street was closed, and Percy Bass was subsequently sold.

Algy's legacy to Percy Bass was his determination to produce and deliver top-quality interior decorating products made by highly skilled craftsmen, employing traditional methods. This dedicated approach continues to this day at Percy Bass, largely thanks to the person who eventually took over the business from Algernon Asprey – Jane Morris. **PB**

The makers' mark of Algernon Asprey.

Below: Door furniture for state rooms from the Al Nassiria Palace, Riyadh.

Jane Morris in the Percy Bass upholstery workshop.

JANE MORRIS

Following a meeting with Algernon Asprey's son Edward in the late 1970s, Jane Morris was persuaded to work for Percy Bass. Jane had just returned from opening a jewellery shop in Muscat, Oman, where she had bought the stock, organised staff appointments and arranged the opening party. Previously, she had worked in the jewellery department at Asprey & Co. for three years, latterly as a buyer, while simultaneously studying gemmology at the Sir John Cass College. At the time, Asprey was supplying many Middle Eastern customers, including the Sultan of Oman.

Edward Asprey no doubt appreciated Jane's ability to deal with clients, as well as her sterling qualifications. She had studied English and History of Art at university, before working at Sotheby's on New Bond Street. Here, she became the first female sales clerk, recording the transactions and bidding for purchasers who did not wish to be recognised in the auction room. Through this role, Jane acquainted herself with all the top antique dealers in London, which proved to be very useful when she moved into the interior decorating business.

When Jane joined Percy Bass, the front of the premises at 188 Walton Street was not a shop, but was used as a thoroughfare to get to the factory and workrooms in Crescent Place. At the time, Percy Bass's main customers were other decorators or designers, and people in affiliated trades. Jane changed the Walton Street entrance, and made it into a shop to attract retail customers to Percy Bass.

Jane looks back to those early days with fond memories

Gradually, Jane built up the retail business by doing everything herself – from one-finger typing, to working out estimates and completing the design assignments. As a result of her own independent commissions, Jane also undertook projects with Edward Asprey, in conjunction with Algernon Asprey's Bruton Street decorating business. One of her first projects was Purley Hall in Pangbourne for the Ali-Reza family. By building up her own customer base, Jane Morris ensured that the Percy Bass decorating business began to flourish.

A FRESH SWEEP
Not long after Jane joined the company, Percy Bass became part of Asprey & Co. of

Percy Bass's interior designers in the 1990s. Clockwise, from left: Christel Helman, Georgina Orde, Rachel Grant-Goodey, Ana Martinez, Jane Morris, Laura Morant, Ishbel Fleming-Boyd and Tomke Becker.

Bond Street. At this stage, Algernon's day-to-day involvement with Percy Bass had become quite limited, and the management of the upholstery and curtain workshops had become somewhat lax. It was not long before this state of affairs became apparent to John Asprey and his colleagues in Bond

Jane really enjoys her job and the business. It has been a life's work

Street, and they decided that a 'new broom' approach was necessary. Asprey's knew and trusted Jane from her days in their jewellery department, so they approached her and asked if she would take on the management of Percy Bass. She agreed, and became manager of the manufacturing unit as well as the shop.

Managing Percy Bass was a whole new world for Jane, as it not only involved

maintaining the company's high standards of workmanship and reliability, but also meant that she had to manage the factory staff as well. The additional responsibility involved tasks such as breaking up fist-fights between the upholsterers, resisting the demands of the trades unions and being 'Auntie Jane' to the seamstresses (most of whom were at least twice her age). Although it was difficult on occasions, Jane still has fond memories of those early days, particularly of the staff who were the highly skilled backbone of Percy Bass.

When Asprey's was restructured in 1982, Jane purchased Percy Bass with a partner. The partnership turned out to be deeply unsatisfactory and, following acrimonious litigation in 1985, it was dissolved. Jane took sole control of the business. Since then, she has built up Percy Bass to have the global reputation it enjoys today. This has been achieved by getting goods made at the right price and quality. This is especially important at the top end of the market, where clients appreciate attention

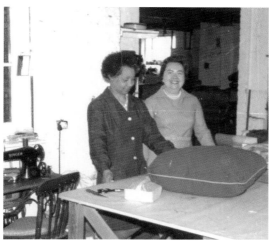

eighties. Another key employee was the estimator, Bill Pearl, who could sketch a design for furniture or curtains in a matter of minutes. These designs were then shown to clients for their approval, and became the specification from which the workshop produced the required items. Jane remembers sitting by a swimming pool at a palace in northern Portugal, and watching Bill produce a detailed sketch of the building which he gave to the grateful owner, Colin Clark.

Customers of the curtain-making and upholstery departments at Percy Bass range from the royal family at Kensington Palace, to pop stars, a royal yacht and an Oscar-winning actor's London home. Over the years, there have been some moments of frustration, such as carrying out all the preparatory work on the design for the Lord Chancellor's flat, only to be obstructed by public officials. But most importantly, there has been lots of laughter. Jane once found herself having to climb over a high wall wearing a miniskirt, having been accidentally locked in the grounds of a house owned by a foreign king.

FROM STRENGTH TO STRENGTH

With the combination of the manufacturing skills base of Percy Bass, its full range of pattern books and decorative accessories, along with Jane's friendly approach, the business continued to grow. Clients were now appearing from all over the world, so Jane decided to recruit a team of young designers to handle the increasing number of decorating commissions.

Since the 1980s, Percy Bass has mainly worked in residential design, with many of the projects based abroad. These have ranged from decorating a house for a Danish businessman in Hong Kong, to a hideaway in the Virgin Islands for an Australian customer. City clients have been especially prominent, commissioning projects such as a house for the head of a leading investment bank in Locust Valley, New York, Morgan Stanley's London town house and the Scottish home of an English banking family.

Much of Percy Bass's work has been on the east coast of America, as well as in

to detail. Percy Bass's approach to design is down-to-earth and hands on, and is always combined with an enthusiastic attitude.

RETAIL EXPANSION

In the early 1980s, Percy Bass purchased the premises at 184 and 186 Walton Street from Macolin, a gift shop that sold children's books and fancy goods. The new, wide frontage allowed Percy Bass to start selling a range of decorative home accessories to augment its upholstery, curtain, fabric and wallpaper lines. This additional range proved to be remarkably popular with retail customers.

Jane inherited one of Percy Bass's great assets when she bought the business: its dedicated and highly skilled workforce. A wonderful Jamaican lady called Hyacinth Stephenson was in charge of the curtain workshop. She had the incredible ability to turn rags into riches. Hyacinth was assisted by a team of ladies, all of whom were expert curtain makers. They have all long since retired, and are now in their

Over the past 30 years, Jane has taught the art of interior decorating to several apprentices

Germany, Denmark, Sweden, Norway and England. Over the years, the fashion for interiors has changed from chintz to tea stain linens, to minimalism, but Jane has always strived to maintain traditional excellence. However, not all of Percy Bass's work has involved residential properties. Commercial commissions have included a conference centre at Brocket Hall and a hotel in Denmark. Merchant banks, especially American investment banks, have also asked Percy Bass to provide their office decorations.

To fully utilise Percy Bass's extensive Walton Street and Crescent Place premises, Jane encouraged some of the company's suppliers to move into the Percy Bass building as tenants. Other companies with related skills followed, so gradually, a creative team of skilled craftsmen was assembled on site. Jane's foresight in supporting relatively unusual skills has, in some cases, kept businesses alive. Jane also liked to support artists by letting studios to them. These artists included Sasha Newley, the son of Joan Collins, and the portrait painter Binny Matthews.

MAINTAINING TRADITIONS

By forging close links with the suppliers that became tenants in the Percy Bass building, the company has been able to maintain its philosophy of including high-quality traditional products and skills in its design projects. These businesses have prospered due to a reliable source of work from Percy Bass. And even though most are no longer located on the Percy Bass premises, they remain stalwart suppliers to the company.

Over the past 30 years, Jane has taught the art of interior decorating to several apprentices, many of whom now have their own successful businesses. These protégées include Ina Lindeman, Cynthia Clarry, Rachel Grant-Goodey, Lady Birdie Fortescue, Philippa Devas and The Hon, April Russell.

Despite the development of an internationally successful decorating business, Percy Bass continues to make curtains and upholstery for other decorators such as Nicholas Haslam. Through being a supplier to other decorators, Percy Bass's

impeccable workmanship has been appreciated by a broad spectrum of discerning customers, ranging from Sir Mick Jagger to Princess Michael of Kent.

When asked what has changed over the last 25 years, Jane immediately responds that clients want everything done immediately. They do not have the time or the patience to wait for their designs, as they would have done in the past. This puts extra pressure on staff but, somehow, everything still seems to be delivered on time. Jane thrives on pressure – she worked until 8 o'clock on the nights that her children were born, and was back at her desk two days later, having created a nursery at the company's premises. The room is still called 'Charlie's bedroom' and, although it is no longer used by the children, they love to come to Percy Bass and lend a hand.

Jane thoroughly enjoys her job and is passionate about the business. Though it has been a life's work, it has been great fun working on an enormous range of different projects and helping give wonderful clients pleasure from their homes. **PB**

Opposite: Neutrals are effective in this room with vibrant art, broken by the coral Eaton check cushions by Colefax & Fowler.

Above: The drawing room at Brocket Hall, decorated in the 1980s by Ina Lindeman of Percy Bass.

Percy Bass acquired 184 and 186 Walton Street in the early 1980s, so the retail side of the company left 188 Walton Street then and moved into the larger shop premises. Number 188 reverted to being an entrance to the factory and workshops in Crescent Place. The ground floor factory space became a showroom for Percy Bass's upholstery, and also displayed a selection of furniture from other suppliers.

As at 188 Walton Street, Jane Morris continued to greet every customer to the shop. As trade increased, she trained and recruited additional members of staff, who were given prime responsibility for shop sales.

With larger retail premises, the range of decorative accessories on offer at Percy Bass grew, as did the number of suppliers. The company became a valued customer for certain suppliers, especially those crafting handmade items to Percy Bass's unique specifications.

of pattern books on display in the Percy Bass shop.

Below: Items with a pug motif are a popular choice.

> As at 188 Walton Street, Jane Morris continues to greet every customer to the shop

THE SHOP

The shop prides itself on its ability to provide unique finishing touches to support any design scheme

Above left: Leather decorative accessories are increasingly popular. In the foreground is a faux fur throw.

Above right: A selection of pattern books.

Jane discovered that offering decorative accessories that were not available elsewhere was an extremely effective way of attracting new customers to the decorating and manufacturing side of the business. She started to devote more time to identifying new products, whilst nurturing craftsmen who could make exactly what Percy Bass, or its customers, wanted. Jane was of the opinion that the bigger the shop range, the more likely it would be to attract a new customer, or keep the existing ones coming back. Thus, Percy Bass acquired the unique appearance of a shop crammed full of goods, with hardly any room for customers.

The entire building was renovated and enlarged in 2004, so the retail and decorating businesses moved to 184 Walton Street. Jane again placed her desk at the front of the shop and, with a bigger sales area, the range of decorative accessories was expanded further. As before, every square inch of floor and wall space is used to display the products, so the shop retains the character of a stylish bazaar. At the rear, there is an even more impressive collection of fabric and pattern books than was available at the original premises. These books remain crucial to Percy Bass's main business of design and decoration. With many sizes and colourful bindings, the books add to the shop's eccentric and eclectic character.

FULL TO THE BRIM

Visiting the Percy Bass shop at 184 Walton Street can be something of a challenge, as there is very little space to move around. Waste paper bins, magazine racks, tissue box holders and trays are stacked precariously, almost to the ceiling. However, if you want something on the bottom of the pile it is never a problem, as stock is constantly shifted around. Percy Bass specialises in customisations. If an item is blue and you want it in green, or personalised with your dog's photograph, this can be made up and delivered within three weeks.

Most of the stock has been designed to coordinate with classic interiors

Above: A cachepot from the Percy Bass shop.

Percy Bass has accounts with virtually every fabric, wallpaper and trimming company in the country, so if a book is not available in store it can be ordered. There is a good cross section of sample books on display so that customers can build design schemes around weaves, silks, cottons, plains and patterns, chenilles, linens, velvets, embroidered fabrics, damasks and chintzes – the list is seemingly endless. The books reflect the Percy Bass business, and include most Colefax & Fowler and Zoffany publications. Fabrics and wallpapers are sourced from all over the world, especially from France and the United States. Despite the exclusivity of its suppliers, Percy Bass is careful to cater for all budgets, so that everyone can enjoy the immense product range offered in the store.

Although interior decorating, upholstery and curtain-making form the largest part of the Percy Bass business, the company is now equally well known for its stylish decorative accessories, many of which are relatively inexpensive and exclusively made. The company never advertises, so many customers are first introduced to Percy Bass through its shop. The shop prides itself on its ability to provide unique finishing touches to support any design scheme. Waste paper bins and tissue boxes, which come in many styles, are available in any colour and can be decorated with a range of designs. Customers often have their accessories customised to match a particular wallpaper or a fabric.

CUSTOMISED COVERS

Percy Bass stocks an extensive range of single and double letter racks, magazine racks and umbrella stands. These can all be produced in a variety of colours, and can also be coordinated to complement a specific design scheme. Surplus fabric from curtains, or a client's own fabric, can be used to cover a bin, notice-board or tissue box holder.

Percy Bass also has an extensive range of cachepots and planters, which can be ordered in a range of sizes to cater to personal requirements. These are ideal for plants, post or pot pourri. There is also an extensive range of trays – from metal ones with fruit and vegetables printed on them for kitchen use, to small black trays with printed animals, suitable for a bottle of water on a bedside table. Other trays have messages such as 'Tea for Two', 'Cappuccino or Espresso', and 'Life is a game, but Bridge is serious' (the latter découpaged with playing cards). It is also popular to have wedding invitations printed on trays as a novel gift. Customers often bring in photographs of their pets, family or sports to have these images transferred onto Percy Bass accessories. Few shops offer this level of custom service.

There are plenty of ideas for the home on display at the Percy Bass shop, so it is well worth spending some time browsing the piles of small pictures.

Amongst these practical objects are some wacky pieces, such as the personalised loo seats made by a supplier called Lulu. These seats have photographs inserted on the top and underside of the lid. Slightly saucier pictures can even be put on the underside of the seat. Personalised orders have included a customer who wanted a seat customised with pictures of her ex-husband's face!

It is often difficult to shop for men, but at Percy Bass there is a range of desktop accessories in the form of book spines, including pencil pots, paper weights, remote control holders, letter racks, ice buckets and box files. Decorative book spines made of resin are also available by the metre. These facades are very realistic, and can be used to conceal a door, line a lift or even to add interest to a wall. It is possible for customers to choose books by title, author or subject, or the spines can be randomly selected. Percy Bass will even include the occasional small horizontal book, for extra authenticity.

Opposite: Ceramic cachepots, ornaments and decorative objects.

Below: Horse book ends support antique leather books.

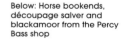

Below: Horse bookends, découpage salver and blackamoor from the Percy Bass shop

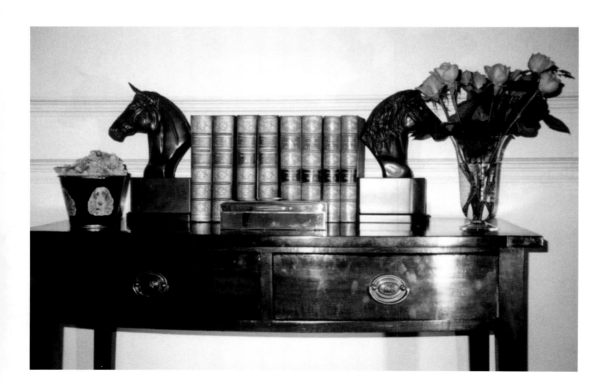

BESPOKE GOODS

The most individual presents available at the shop are the message cushions, which come in a selection of styles and fabrics. Needlepoint cushions can be customised with pictures of various breeds of dog, or any other motif, to order. Alternatively, cushions with slogans such as, 'If you want the best seat in the house, move the cat', 'Men, coffee and chocolate are all better rich' can be ordered, along with pink and blue mini cushions for babies. Moiré or velvet cushions with rope edging are another option and, again, any slogan can be added at the customer's request.

More expensive additions to decorative themes can always be ordered from Percy Bass. The company has accounts with most major suppliers. Orders have included bespoke picture frames, mirrors, lamps and an assortment of curtain poles with various finials. Due to the lack of space in the shop, Percy Bass cannot display many samples of larger products, but there are many examples of smaller pieces of furniture in lower price ranges.

Percy Bass also stocks contemporary items. These products are made of materials like rattan or wicker, and include items such as work trays, pen pots, picnic baskets with compartments for wine, tissue boxes and bins. Leather is also popular, sometimes in the form of cow hide (often called pony skin), and is used to cover pieces such as photo frames and ice buckets. Another popular material is fake fur, which is stocked in a variety of colours. This material makes appealing hot water bottle covers and bed throws, which can also have a choice of lining fabrics to match an existing design scheme.

Most of the stock has been designed to coordinate with classic interiors, adding easily assembled finishing touches. This can involve table-top ornaments, such as candlesticks and ceramic objects.

If your dog needs something more indulgent than a personalised cushion or a matching bin, then it could have its own découpaged cream rack for leads, complete with its own photo glazed onto the centre of a ceramic bowl. When leaving the shop and closing the door, you may just remember that you need a doorstop. These are available in brass, cast iron or resin, and are shaped as horses or pigs, painted scenes, rugby boots or shoes.

Though it might sometimes resemble a frantic bazaar, the Percy Bass shop is undoubtedly the ultimate emporium for decadent, traditional homeware. **PB**

Left: Not all of Percy Bass decoration is domestic. A contemporary office designed for a Chair-woman. The paint is Farrow & Ball's blue/green and the faux leopard skin cushion fabric is from Kravat.

Opposite: A typical Percy Bass message cushion, cachepot and waste paperbin. Check cushion and curtains are in Colefax & Fowler fabric.

The interior design business has changed remarkably over the last 25 years

INTERIOR DECORATION

S ince the original business was centred around making high-quality curtains and upholstered furnishings on the premises, it was only natural that Percy Bass would eventually provide a complete interior design service.

Over the years, many of the interior shops that had their own workrooms have gradually disappeared, particularly in the fashionable areas of London. By adding desirable accessories and unlimited pattern books throughout the shop, Percy Bass has expanded its business – and secured its future.

The interior design business has changed remarkably over the last 25 years. Firstly, it has become more flexible, allowing more choice. Today, a designer can be involved in any aspect of a project, from decorating to dealing with architects, builders and structural engineers, as well as arranging the final ornaments. Secondly, clients are now much more design conscious and regularly read interior magazines and books for current trends and inspiration.

By using a professional interior decorator, clients can be guided in their personal aspirations and ideas, while avoiding mistakes. The coordinating skills of a designer can be a great help to those with hectic lifestyles. The client can still retain control of individual preferences and manage an

Opposite and above: Classic decoration in earth tones for this London flat. The table is by Carew Jones.

Inset: A collection of contemporary accessories completes the theme.

overview of the desired look. Some clients collect wallpaper and fabric cuttings, and then seek help to put it all together. This leaves the decorator free to advise on the best window treatments, the perfect paint colour and the optimum floor coverings for the space in question.

THE WAY FORWARD IS THE WAY BACK

Style no longer follows a rigid format. There are still examples of Queen Anne, Georgian, Victorian, Art Nouveau, Edwardian and Art Deco design, but they tend to be individual pieces of furniture, ornaments or colours used to complement the twenty-first century home.

There is no doubt that an historic house would need to be redecorated in total sympathy with its original features. However, most people move home frequently, changing their ideas about the way they live. Interior decorators have to enthusiastically reflect the professional and domestic lifestyles of their clients. These changes now happen faster than ever before, so clients expect prompt delivery, as well as high quality.

The planning stage is crucial to any decorative scheme. It usually begins with proper consideration of the architectural elements of a room.

A desk arranged with personal objects, books, photographs and flowers.

Opposite, above: a classic study in understated elegance. Bookcases, desk, chair and stool by David Linley. Curtains are in Bennison's Ponticherry.

Opposite, below: The lime greens and peach tones of the picture are picked up by the bowl of fruit in this town house dining room.

Above: The beige toile wallpaper is Mount Vernon by Brunschwig & Fils; the chair upholstery is made from fabrics from Manuel Canovas. Sepia prints blend well with the beige toile.

A large proportion of the work carried out by Percy Bass is based in central London, which is dominated by Victorian buildings. There are also many red brick buildings, which have been converted into flats. These buildings usually have white window frames, bay windows and black wrought ironwork balconies. Central London also features stucco and stock brick terraced houses with parapets. These are generally well built, and have beautifully proportioned, adaptable living spaces. The decorator's job is to transform these residences into comfortable and pleasurable homes that accommodate today's style of living and entertaining. This might include replacing cornices, dado rails, doors and door furniture, architraves and skirting boards that had previously been ripped out. These original features were often removed in the 1960s and 1970s, in an attempt to modernise interiors. As part of this movement, fireplaces were usually covered over and ceilings lowered. Thankfully, the vandalisation of historic buildings has come to an end, as today's planning regulations are conscious of protecting architectural heritage.

INFORMAL SEATING

Once the building elements of the design process have been finalised, the decorator can begin to plan furniture layouts. It is important to know exactly how much space a client

As a general rule, the larger the room, the less decoration it needs

needs for entertaining, or for children. In a traditional room, seating areas should be based around a focal point, such as a fireplace. In larger rooms, the establishment of two or three seating areas creates a comfortable look. It is practical to place occasional tables near seating, as long as there are not too many exposed legs on show; this can make a room look cluttered. This potential problem can be avoided by using circular, skirted tables with a floor-length cloth, with optional bullion fringe. A more contemporary storage alternative is to place a small trunk beside a seating area. An upholstered stool can enhance a room, and also serve a variety of purposes. It can be used as a tray, for books or as occasional seating. Likewise, a club fender by the fireplace can be used as a perch, and also lends an air of informality to a classic drawing room.

If a client already has antique furniture and pictures, then a neutral background is ideal, as it allows the beauty of the contents to impose their own character on a room. This style of under-stated decoration creates a timeless, somewhat 'undecorated' look. Collecting antiques

need not involve the exclusive selection of 'brown' furniture. A beautiful walnut bureau bookcase can look stunning, but a room full of similar wood looks unimaginative and can seem like a poor attempt to replicate eighteenth-century style. By mixing traditional English pieces with items of French furniture

Top: A contemporary bedroom with curtains by Warner & Son.

Above: A roman blind in Rubelli's 'pirates' sets the scene for this girl's bedroom.

and decorative accessories, a client can create a far more interesting look. French console tables or cabinets look stunning in any room, as do a pair of French fauteuil chairs. These pieces are particularly at home in a contemporary setting. Modern rooms can also benefit from the addition of chinoiserie. Whether of English or Chinese origin, the addition of screens, cabinets or tray tables can add an extra dimension to a room, especially if it also features Oriental porcelain.

Blue and white Chinese porcelain looks striking in any setting, while the colours of Japanese Arita wares, such as Imari and Katani, work particularly well in neutral surroundings. Tall vases can be made into lamps, and although there are many reproductions on the market, they cannot compare with the quality of a genuine antique piece. In a large room, a lidded baluster vase can look more powerful and less cluttered than a series of smaller ornaments.

LESS IS MORE

As a general rule, the larger the room, the less decoration it needs. A few over-scaled pieces of furniture will have more impact than smaller items. Tiny, angular rooms benefit from matching wallpaper and curtain fabric, which help to disguise

Keep modern rooms looking fresh by updating items such as lamps, lampshades and coffee tables

architectural flaws. Contrary to popular opinion, rooms with little natural light, such as basements, can be given character by using dark wallpapers and plenty of lighting. At night, the effect is warm and cosy, and by day the décor in the room is given clarity by low-voltage ceiling lighting. This is especially effective if tiny bulbs are angled onto pieces of fine art.

Opposite: Dining room with reclaimed oak floors and stone architraves has a mixture of oak and French walnut furniture. The porcelain is Portuguese.

Above: A collection of blue and white porcelain has been deliberately arranged with two prints depicting similar pots.

However, not all properties have an architectural heritage that will support a traditional design scheme. There are plenty of blocks of flats, such as those built between the 1960s and 1970s, that are quite featureless. These buildings often need more help with soft features, such as full curtains and comfortable furnishings. To ensure that modern rooms look fresh, it is important to update items that quickly go out of fashion. These include lamps, lampshades and coffee table styles. A room can also be rejuvenated by the introduction of contemporary ornaments and cushions.

Working as an interior decorator at Percy Bass is an absolute pleasure, as everything that you might need is on-hand. It is a priceless advantage to have the company's dedicated upholstery, furniture restoration, French polishing, bespoke furniture, passementerie, carpeting and graphic design facilities all in the

same building, or close by. When a client wants to discuss whether to finish a fine upholstered chair in double piping, braid or antiqued nails, the designer can simply take them to the upholstery workshop, where they can see every stage of the process. This speeds up the decision-making and, consequently, the design process.

Percy Bass has built up an unrivalled list of contacts over the decades, ensuring that virtually any piece of furniture or object can be sourced, or copied. The versatility and professionalism of the interior designers at Percy Bass helps clients to avoid decorating pitfalls. Whether an order relates to one pair of curtains or the design scheme for an entire house, Percy Bass's suppliers and support services use traditional skills to make the finest quality products, in the minimum amount of time. **PB**

Above: A circular table is an ideal way to give character to an empty corner of a room.

Opposite: A Chinese export table top cupboard is enhanced with oriental porcelain and a cinnibar box. The curtain fabric is by Colefax & Fowler.

UPHOLSTERY

The traditional method of covering seat furniture is to use a filling of horsehair or fibre, sew springs on and add cushions with a feather and down filling. Every aspect is constructed by hand, rather than using mass-produced foam rubber or patent springing.

At Percy Bass, upholstered seating is still made to these exacting traditional standards. The company is one of the few businesses of its kind to employ such methods. Whether an order is to restore and strip down an eighteenth-century fauteuil in need of refurbishment after 200 years of use, or to create a modern chair covered in Alcantara, the manufacture process is exactly the same.

Upholstered seating is still made to exacting, traditional standards

Customers often cut out a photograph of a sofa in a magazine and ask for an exact copy, or they may already have a favourite sofa and want another to make a pair. The designers at Percy Bass begin by creating a scale drawing that is then given to the frame makers, H Vaughan Ltd.

Vaughan's take the scale drawings and make beech frames, with wood imported from Germany. They still use the traditional dowel method (two-inch

Opposite: Chair covered in a Pierre Frey fabric, with cushion fabric from Manuel Canovas. The lively wall colour is Farrow & Ball's Lulworth Blue and the curtains are a hot pink silk taffeta from Osborne & Little.

Above: A traditional sofa covered by Percy Bass in fabric from Manuel Canovas. The curtains and cushions are a Colefax & Fowler linen called Lyndhurst.

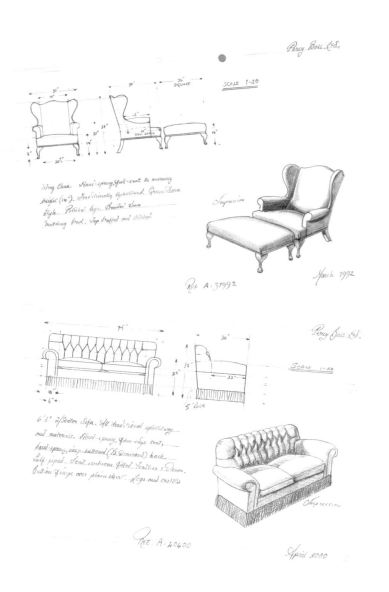

long rods made of wood) for furniture joints. The frame is then delivered to Percy Bass's dedicated upholsterer, Candido de Silva (or it may go to Rich Restoration if the specifications stipulate stained or polished legs). Candido has spent his whole life as an upholsterer, and used to drive around London in a white taxi customised with leather, button-back seats with curtains and an accordion-pleated ceiling. He loves to work in the traditional way, ensuring that every piece he produces is of the highest quality. This furniture will not only keep its shape, but also give long-lasting service.

TRADITIONAL METHODS

In the 1930s, when Percy Bass ran his own upholstery workshop at Walton Street, most department stores had their own upholstery-making departments. These stores included Whiteley's of Bayswater, John Barker of Kensington and Waring & Gillow of Hammersmith. In those days, the learning process for upholsterers consisted of a three-year apprentice-ship, followed by a year as an 'improver', before becoming a fully-fledged, professional upholsterer.

Above: Scale drawings of a wing chair and a button back sofa with bullion fringe (sketched by Bill Pearl).

Right: A jean-stitched suede sofa. Fabric by Mary Fox Linton, cushions by Etro and Rubelli.

Opposite: Covers, bolsters and cushions for a day bed. Fabrics are Andrew Martin's, Magna Carta and York.

Below: Cushions, from left to right, rabbit skin from Andrew Martin, De Le Cuoña's suede, Abbot & Boyd's Cinnibar and Claremont's Amore Canali.

Upholstering is a complex
art that requires many years
of specialist expertise

Above: This cosy room has a sofa and chair covered in Bennison's Tiger Lily. The faux leopardskin fabric on the bergère is by GP & J Baker and offsets the florals.

Opposite: A custom-made Percy Bass sofa in a neutral setting.

Below: Candido working on an antique chair.

Upholstering starts with a hessian base that is nailed to the lower edge of the frame, ready for the addition of coil springs. These springs, which were invented in the early nineteenth century, are sewn to the webbing using upholsterer's twine. The filling used is a mixture of simulated horsehair underneath, with real horsehair on the surface, all of which is stitched in place by hand. Modern materials have to comply with fire regulations, so Percy Bass is careful to ensure that traditional crafts meet today's strict safety standards.

If the furniture in question is antique, Percy Bass will apply a final layer of calico lining before finishing the piece in the customer's own fabric. There is a choice of double-piping, braid or nails for the finished edging. Piping is popular, even on older pieces of furniture, but close nailed edging, using French brass nails from Claremont, is a more traditional look. A decorative alternative is to braid the edges with spaced nails.

THE FINISHING TOUCHES

To create a bespoke sofa or armchair, the customer has to make many decisions about the finishing touches required at the base edge. There are many alternatives, such as whether to have a gathered skirt, with or without coordinating edging; to keep it plain; to have kick pleats at the front corners; or to have box pleating or a bullion fringe. The customer also has to decide which filling to use for the cushions on the

Left: A country cottage atmosphere in this London mews house, sofa covered in Titley & Marr and accessories from the Percy Bass shop – designed by Jennie Elias of Percy Bass.

Opposite: The Roman blind is in Jane Churchill's Trailing Leaf. The headboard is Colefax & Fowler's Pelham Check. Foreground cushions – left, Jean Munro's Ivory House; right, sheepskin cushion by Conran.

sofa. There is a choice of feather and down (standard mix is 25 per cent down), down and feather (50/50), 100 per cent down or Dacron wrapped. Finally, there is a choice of styles for the seam edges, which can be plain, cord, piped or contrast piped. Loose covers can also be made, and are usually cut in the customer's home and brought back to the workshop to be sewn. These covers contain zips. For traditional Chesterfield sofas, chaise longues or bedroom chairs, a button-back finish may be required. Buttons can be covered in a variety of fabrics and although this process is lengthy, it certainly has lasting appeal.

Percy Bass can also upholster headboards in any shape or size. The board is cut to shape, with a fixing for either a bed or wall attachment. The board can be custom-made, with varieties of covering including rouched or plain borders, plain-piped or button-back. French padded head-boards are upholstered in the same way as a chair would be.

To create the perfect finishing touch, a few handmade cushions help to make a room look comfortable. These can be made up in any fabric and are usually edged with piping, rope or tassels. If a customer already has an old piece of tapestry, this can be repaired, or needlepoint is often brought into the workshop and stretched into shape, ready to be made into a cushion.

To make squab cushions that fit the shape of a chair, upholsterers generally begin by making a template that is cut out to form a box edge, with piped seams. Rope piping can then be hand-stitched or flanged (rope on a tape, which can be machine stitched, and is therefore less expensive), or leather can be applied with saddle-stitch. The traditional way to make squabs (the oldest style of cushion, dating back to medieval times) is to use horsehair edged with felt. This traditional method of upholstery coordinates beautifully with antique furniture.

Chaise longues often have bolsters to complement the classical look. These can also be filled with horsehair or a feather and down mix. The bolsters are then hand stitched, with pleated or plain ends, and are finished with a button or tassel.

Candido works with many different styles of fabrics – from silks, tapestries, wool weaves, jacquards, chintzes and cottons, to leather and suede – but if he had to choose a personal favourite, it would be the old damasks and Fortuny silks. **PB**

CURTAINS & BLINDS

Percy Bass only makes bespoke curtains. They are crafted in a traditional fashion, exactly as they were when the decorating business began nearly 100 years ago.

Chris O'Reilly started work as a curtain fitter for Percy Bass in the 1980s. In those days, curtains were still being made in the Walton Street factory, with Hyacinth Stevenson, master curtain maker, in charge. The curtains are no longer made on the premises, but Chris still does all the estimates and has extensive experience in the trade.

The original workroom at Percy Bass was very old-fashioned, with a stove in the corner of the room that had to be lit every morning. Work only began when the room warmed up a little. Unlike today, there was never any rush; curtain makers were asked when a pair of curtains would be finished, rather than being told when they had to be ready. Curtains and swags would often be made up in calico, to make sure that

Right: A London blind is an attractive alternative to a fuller festoon blind. This example also has a roman blind in a different fabric underneath.

Opposite: Bennison's English Toile, made to a special inky red colour on an oyster background, in contrast to the blue and white of the Chinese porcelain.

the client liked them. If the client was unhappy with any aspect of the design, the mock-up could be altered. In this day and age, quick delivery is essential to accommodate busy lifestyles, so Percy Bass ensures that a pair of curtains is ready two weeks after receipt of the fabric.

SPECIFIC TAILORING

Percy Bass decorators advise clients about specific curtains, interpreting their ideas and requirements. They use the benefit of their experience to comment on the suitability of a particular style for a certain shape of window. For example, the

decorators will discuss whether to have a fan edge or a heavy bullion fringe on a pelmet and also debate the relative merits of an edging border on a roman blind.

Chris believes that curtain styles have come full circle. When he started in the 1980s, the trend was to have buckram-shaped pelmets. They have now come back into fashion, but today's pelmets tend to be padded and upholstered. Manufacturing techniques have improved meanwhile; for example, buckram is no longer used, as it had a habit of warping (particularly if there was a hot radiator underneath the window).

In this day
and age,
quick delivery
is essential to
accommodate
busy lifestyles

Swags and tails are still in demand, but
tend to be used in a softer, less formal
style. Contemporary fashion favours eyelet
curtains on poles and cartridge-style
headings (which are like a small goblet
pleat). Pinch pleating has also stood the
test of time, as this heading allows
curtains to hang in attractive folds. Percy
Bass curtains are always hand gathered
and pleated – tapes are never used.

WINDOW DRESSING

Roman blinds are currently extremely
popular, as their simple elegance suits a
variety of window shapes. They have an
added advantage, as they can incorporate
blackout lining for bedrooms, which keeps
out early-morning light and ensures a good
night's sleep. This lining also conceals the
integral rods in strong sunlight. Another
style that has all but disappeared is the
Austrian, or festoon, blind. This type of
blind has been popular since the mid-
eighteenth century and, as styles are so
often cyclical, will probably make a
comeback in the near future. At the
moment, the less bulbous London blind
seems to be a more popular option.

Decorators use the benefit of their experience to comment on the suitability of a particular style for a certain shape of window

Percy Bass only employs traditional methods to make curtains and blinds; absolutely everything is handmade to fulfil specific client requirements. For example, there are five different weights of interlining to choose from; these are carefully selected to suit the job in question. Lighter fabrics need heavier interlinings, so Percy Bass assesses each project individually.

Additional features, such as smocking and covered buttons, are also made by hand. Prior to attachment, the weights for the curtain hems are sewn into little bags and chain loops are placed at every seam, to ensure that the curtain and its lining stay perfectly in place. In addition to these quality measures, all curtain edges are surged and the interlinings are herringbone stitched to the fabric.

TIMELESS DRAPERY

In addition to curtains and blinds, Percy Bass also makes other soft furnishing items, including bedcovers, bed valances and drapes for four-poster beds. If bedcovers need to be quilted, they are sent to a specialist, such as Louis Moreau. (See p148).

Chintz fabrics remain popular for traditional country homes, but in more modern settings the fashion has swung towards fabrics such as animal prints, simulated suede and natural linens. Generally, curtains have become more tailored and less fussy, favouring cleaner lines.

Style is constantly evolving, and Percy Bass's curtain team always adapt accordingly. Although the current trend is for simple and tailored curtains, the curtain-making process continues to be carried out in the traditional way, ensuring that the company retains its reputation for quality, regardless of the capricious demands of fashion. **PB**

Below: A stylish roman blind contrast-piped in red for the dining area of a kitchen.

Persian carpets laid on top of a fitted velvet pile carpet can define areas in a very large room.

CARPETS & RUGS

When an interior designer embarks on a project, the largest area for consideration is the floor space. Selecting an appropriate floor covering for rooms, hallways, stairs and landings is a vital decision, which will eventually enhance the whole design scheme.

Percy Bass can supply any floor covering – from a budget carpet for a rental property, to a custom-made, silk and wool, velvet pile Wilton. Carpets and rugs can be sourced from all over the world, but over half of Percy Bass's clients ask for their floor coverings to be designed individually.

The carpet department is where Peter Colbourn, the carpet expert, works alongside his son, Toby. Peter and his team of fitters can advise on all aspects of floor covering and are especially experienced in selecting the appropriate quality, colourway, pattern and texture for any given design scheme.

Wooden floors are also very popular, rendered in both modern materials and reclaimed boards. These floors are usually coupled with antique or modern rugs, which can be sourced or custom-made to any specification or design.

COLOURFUL CREATIONS

Custom-made carpets can be manufactured on narrow-width, either 27 inches (69cm) or 36 inches (91cm), or broadloom (up to 4m wide, depending on the quantity ordered and the repetition of the pattern). All Percy Bass carpets are woven in England, using traditional methods and the finest materials available. Wilton carpets can be supplied in several forms including velvet-cut pile, loop pile (known as Brussels weave) and textured (which is a mixture of cut and loop with varying heights of loop, or varying heights of cut). Whether narrow or broadloom, the design permutations and colour palettes for carpets are infinite. To further expand the parameters of individualisation, the yarn used can include silk, linen, art silk, rayon and metal.

Carpet design is usually limited to five colours, which is enough to satisfy most needs, although additional colours can now be planted. The design is created on a computer, although the actual carpet is produced on a Jacquard loom, using traditional methods.

Textured carpets are becoming increasingly popular, as varying heights of pile can create interest in a single colour

Wilton is more stable and hard-wearing than Axminster, which is created using a cut-pile-only process, where the tufts are put into the carpet. Axminster also has less wool content, so although it can have the same pile weight as a Wilton carpet above the surface, it always has a quantity of dead yarn underneath.

The weaving of a Brussels carpet is a Wilton process. However, instead of cutting the pile to form a velvet surface, it is woven meticulously. It is a much more complex process and takes longer to weave, so is more expensive. If a customer with a tight budget really wants a large patterned rug with no seams, Percy Bass can provide a hand-tufted rug. This flexible method produces intricate designs in many colours, with a thick, dense pile. The surface has a less regular finish than a machine-made alternative. The tufts, which are fed through a nylon mesh, can be of different weights and are available as plain or stippled yarns. This method can produce up to 39 feet (12m) of carpet.

PILE IT HIGH

Textured carpets are becoming increasingly popular, as varying the height of the pile can make a single-colour carpet more dynamic. These textures can be further enhanced by using various wools, ranging from 100 per cent fine worsted wool to coarser blended yarns. This process looks particularly good on staircases, with suede or leather borders and stair rods. These rods can be supplied in metals such as iron, brushed steel, chrome, nickel, black gunmetal or brass, and are often made to coordinate with antique or modern light fittings. Other popular designs for hall and staircase carpeting are stripes and strié, which can add a striking, contemporary look.

Many carpets require special border treatments. It is best to produce two borders, which are woven in one width and split down the middle, to create two

Above: An embossed wool carpet with coordinated edging and stair rods adds style to this elegant hall.

Opposite: A dramatic entrance is created with a red strié carpet. The walls are painted in Farrow & Ball's String.

A patterned carpet
matches the colour scheme
and the furnishings in this
London drawing room.

Opposite: Curtains by
Pierre Frey, teamed with an
embossed wool carpet.

lengths of border with salvages. These can then be sewn to the edge of the carpet. The border is always mitred at the corners. This is a traditional finishing method that allows the border to be taken around awkward angles. Alternatively, a border can be added using the Chlidema method. This approach is often more precise, as Jacquard cards are cut for both the side and end borders, ensuring that the pile always lies in the same direction. This method is ideal for square or rectangular shapes.

Once a design has been approved, Percy Bass can arrange for a carpet to be ready in six to eight weeks. Trial samples can be made by hand for client approval.

A NEUTRAL BACKDROP

The current trend for wood flooring has recently overtaken requests for sisal and sea grass carpeting, which is less durable and stains easily. However, most clients like to combine wood floors with rugs for extra comfort. These often have to be made to size. Animal skins are popular, and can be printed to resemble patterns such as piebald or skewbald pony skin. The base for these designs is usually cowhide. The rug borders are made of suede or leather, and can be supplied in any colour.

With an overwhelming selection of design options available, almost anything is possible in carpet and rug making. However, despite the vast choice on offer, almost half of Percy Bass's customers still choose neutral beige or taupe in a velvet pile – possibly to provide a suitable backdrop to more imposing furniture or curtains. **PB**

PLANS &
PERSPECTIVES

Left: Plans help clients to see an accurate interpretation of their room.

The most important stage in any interior design scheme is the planning, so accurate scale drawings are vital. The drawings not only show the client the potential furniture layout, but also provide detailed information for builders, plumbers, cabinet makers and electricians. In some cases, the plans can also be used for quantity surveying; for instance, if expensive slabs of marble are to be used for bathrooms or flooring, a surveyor can make accurate costing estimates based on the scale drawings.

John draws perspectives, so that clients have an exact idea of how a room will look when it is finished

John Wilson has been drawing plans for Percy Bass since 1988. He works at a drawing board on the first floor of 184 Walton Street, amongst the interior decorators.

Before John starts working on detailed plans, he goes to the proposed renovation site and spends a few hours measuring the area. The ideal scale to work with is metric 1:50, but for more detailed drawings John uses 1:20.

CLOSE CONSULTATION

For furniture layouts, John uses negative scale drawings, rather than templates. These drawings can be easily rearranged, depending on client requirements. John is frequently asked to draw wardrobe interiors. He carefully

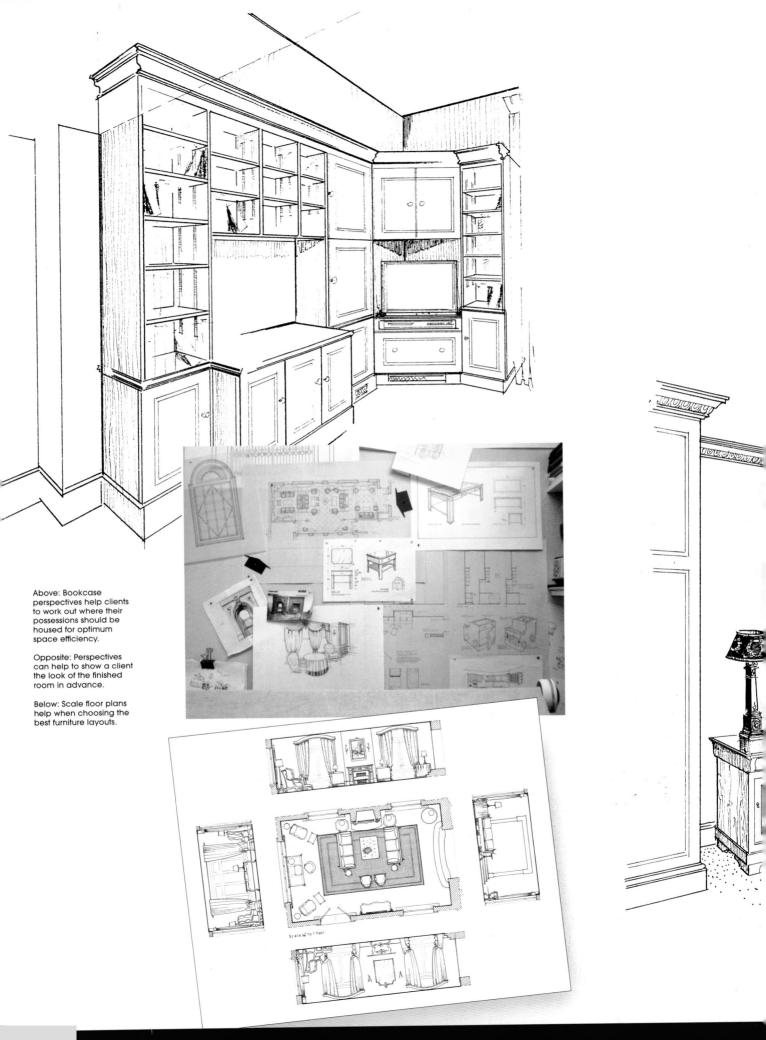

Above: Bookcase
perspectives help clients
to work out where their
possessions should be
housed for optimum
space efficiency.

Opposite: Perspectives
can help to show a client
the look of the finished
room in advance.

Below: Scale floor plans
help when choosing the
best furniture layouts.

Scale ¼" to 1 Foot

works out the details, consulting closely with the decorator. He plans storage space for clothing and accessories, with practical details such as holes in shoe drawers to aid circulation and cut-out handles on drawers for a flush finish.

Another aspect of John's work is to draw perspectives, so that clients have an exact idea of how a room will look when it is finished. These drawings are usually provided in black and white. Although hand tinting is something that John enjoys, this type of drawing is laborious, expensive and delays the completion of a project. When Algernon Asprey owned Percy Bass, colour perspectives were often

Colour perspectives were often painted for large commissions

painted for large commissions. As an accomplished artist, Algy would spend hours painting every proposed room setting for a palace, or landmark property. However, modern delivery times no longer allow for such luxuries.

DOGGED PERSISTENCE
Occasionally, an unusual problem will arrive on John's desk. One such request

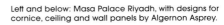

Algernon Asprey's designs

Centre, left and right: Sketch for HM's Office, the main feature of which is the set of six large wall brackets incorporating the Royal Arms.

Below, left and right: Sketch for the entrance hall, Al Nassiria Palace, Riyadh.

was to provide a dog flap for a client's basset hound. Being a cat owner, John's first idea was to draw an enlarged cat flap. He visited the client to measure the substantially built dog (33cm across the chest, 38cm high and an astonishing 94cm long). John proposed that the flap should be activated by the dog pushing it with his nose, but the client was not happy with this arrangement and wanted the

Occasionally, unusual projects occur, such as providing a dog flap for a client's basset hound.

flap to be automatic. Ingeniously, John incorporated an electric car window mechanism into the design, which could be operated via a beam on the dog's collar. This was also unacceptable, as the client thought that it might prove to be a security risk, so John went back to the drawing board. Another device suggested was based on the mechanism of the ambulance gates at Charing Cross Hospital. The

Left: Domestic interiors and specially designed furniture by Algernon Asprey.

Below: Percy Bass solved the unusual request of a mechanical dog flap for a basset hound.

electronic panel could be housed underneath the floorboards, so that the flap would be activated when the dog approached the door with a transmitter around its neck. Again, the client was not convinced, because she worried that the long dog might get its tail trapped in the closing door as it negotiated a rather steep step. The problem was finally solved by using a trigger pad and a light beam. While the beam was interrupted by the tail, or any other part of the dog, the flap would stay open. The doorstep was also shortened so that the dog could easily negotiate his way in and out of the garden.

SHARED TALENTS

The businesses associated with Percy Bass interact with each other to the extent that John often draws plans for the commissioned furniture made by Carew Jones (see p86). John also makes up sample boards of coordinating wallpapers, fabrics and carpets for interior decorators to use in preliminary presentations to Percy Bass clients.

John is also interested in making scale models. He has made models of houses and designer kitchens, but has yet to be asked to make a dolls house; a commission that he would undoubtedly relish. **PB**

DÉCOUPAGE

EEVA CREAL

In her Surrey studio, Eeva Creal makes exquisite découpage accessories for the Percy Bass shop. The workshop is attached to her hilltop home and looks out over a glorious garden that, in summer, is filled with a mass of floribunda rosebushes. This visual backdrop inspires Eeva to create floral motif arrangements, which she then cuts out and glues to all manner of decorative items.

Whereas Caroline de M. Walker decorates black objects with gold coloured relief, Eeva's work predominately features cream crackle glaze. She works exclusively for Percy Bass, and has done so for the past five years. Eeva always has a selection of objects, at varying stages of readiness, and willingly caters for specialist orders, such as those matching a specific fabric or featuring a favourite pet. This kind of bespoke work accounts for about 30 per cent of her output.

A FINE PEDIGREE

Eeva has just finished making a tray with a picture of a customer's racehorse on it, but most of the animal orders are for dogs. Apart from the popular Pugs and Labradors, Eeva occasionally has to provide découpage for unusual breeds, such as Chinese water dogs. Over the years, she has become very knowledge-able about the various breeds, but there is one that she has yet to master – the Lurcher. These dogs are not actually a true pedigree, so there is no accepted standard for them. The name is a loose description for a cross between a whippet and a deer hound.

Eeva has had some bizarre commissions in her time, such as the customer who supplied a photograph of a dog in black and white, but wanted the dog to be brown, or another customer who wanted to have a hand-painted bandana around a dog's neck. Once, Eeva was asked to produce a whole range of accessories with hippos all over them. This was relatively easy to research, but when asked for a particular breed of chicken, she quickly rushed to the local library for help.

Although Eeva loves making the stock ranges, she also enjoys the challenge of being creative and making an item that she has not attempted before. New items and designs are regularly added to Percy Bass stock. Eeva often experiments of her own accord, as she did with the Tea for Two tray, which has proved extremely popular, but Jane Morris also suggests ideas that she thinks the customers might like. One client recently requested a waste paper basket made to look like cardboard. With innate artistic ability, inherited from her Finnish family, Eeva tackles these projects with ease. She even learnt how to make her own paints, under the tutelage of Kevin McCloud and Belinda Ballantine.

Eeva mixes her own colours to create the perfect shade of cream for her découpage, primes and undercoats several times, and then applies top coats.

CUT AND PASTE
Arranging the cut-out pieces and sticking them onto the cream base is not as easy as it looks. It takes a considerable amount of time, and is largely intuitive. A layer of glaze seals the design, and makes the cream colour turn slightly yellow. This is followed by an application of crackle glaze, which is mixed by hand, boiled and then left to cool.

Eeva uses two different oil-based varnishes, which cause a chemical reaction that results in the cracking effect when the glaze dries. This is not an exact process; the size of the cracks depends on the dryness of the first coat, which should be tacky prior to application of the second formula. The cracks are then filled with an oil-based paint, usually Royal Amber, but also dark blue or dark green. The final layers of varnish (there should be at least three)

each need a day to dry, which is why a decorated item can take a long time to make.

Occasionally, Eeva finds objects at local craft and antique fairs, but the majority of her bases come from a range of English suppliers. Once, Eeva ordered some cachepots from India; they mistook centimetres for inches, resulting in the arrival of a batch of giant pots. These have since been used to great effect in her garden, and others have been given to friends.

Découpage is a labour-intensive exercise, so Eeva spends much of her time in the studio. Although she reproduces many pictures of dogs, she does not have one herself. Instead, in a corner of the room, there lies a Burmese cat, napping in a strip of warm sunlight. **PB**

DÉCOUPAGE
CAROLINE DE M. WALKER

T hree distinctive black hatboxes, decorated with floral motifs and ribbon swags, are lined up on a shelf in Caroline de M. Walker's studio. These have been specially commissioned to go alongside a display of antique watering cans in a flower room in Sussex. The cans are made of old French metal and have, in Caroline's words, 'scoopy handles'. Initially,

they are covered in red oxide, as a primer, but will ultimately be highly decorative.

Caroline began specialising in découpage in the early 1990s, and has sold her goods in New York, Los Angeles and Japan. The business was initially based in the Percy Bass building. Students would often come in to be trained, and Charlie (Jane Morris's

Above: Antique and modern base items receive the same treatment.

Opposite: A cream crackle glazed stick or umbrella stand with floral motifs.

son) would drop by to do some painting. Caroline currently works exclusively for the Percy Bass shop, and decorates approximately 500 items each year.

Découpage is the art of decorating surfaces with pieces of cut-out paper. This practice dates back many centuries and can be traced to folk art in the twelfth century. It was also popular with seventeenth-century Venetian cabinet makers, who tried to imitate lacquered wares imported from the Orient. By the eighteenth century, the craft had become a favoured pastime for European nobility. In England, Mrs Mary Delaney (1700–88) became particularly well known for découpage works featuring specimen flowers, and she received many private commissions from the aristocracy, including several from King George III and Queen Charlotte. Some of these magnificent collages contain more than 230 pieces of tinted and cut paper, and many are still exhibited in the British Museum.

DRAWING ROOM PURSUITS
Queen Victoria was a keen collector of découpage, and the craft became a favourite drawing room pastime, as a fresh alternative to watercolour painting or embroidery. Results could be achieved relatively quickly, and the skills required were more instinctive, as opposed to artistic.

Today, the art of découpage is experiencing a revival, due to the advent of laser photocopying, the availability of old prints and improved paint technology.

Queen Victoria was a keen collector of découpage, which became a favourite drawing room pastime

The base objects for découpage can be antique or modern. Caroline is currently decorating tin Victorian cake baskets, a 1920s pewter wash tub, some cachepots, pen holders and modern waste paper baskets.

The most popular lines are waste paper baskets, along with any object that will hold a plant. Small trays, including gallery trays, also sell well as gifts, and can even feature personal messages. About 10 per cent of the items made are special commissions, and those featuring dogs are especially popular. Caroline has books on every breed of dog, and cats too. Labradors are the best-selling dog motif, followed by King Charles Spaniels and Pugs, with a number of terriers close behind.

MUSICAL MOTIFS

The process begins with a coating of red oxide, which is painted onto the object. After 24 hours, two coats of matt blackboard paint are applied. Meanwhile, motifs are cut out from old books (or hand drawn) and are made into a collage, ready for photocopying. These pictures can include bows, dogs, architectural borders, garlands, fruit, hearts, shells, putti, crests, fleur de lys or antlers. Music can also be reproduced – a favourite being Wagner's Bridal March. The master copy is always saved for possible future use.

Once the object has been primed, the motif is stuck to it with a mixture of Unibond and wallpaper paste. At this stage, the artwork must be allowed

sufficient time to dry, or the paper will simply curl up. The paper can then be coloured with a mixture of powdered gold leaf and shellac (a varnish made from bees' wings). To obtain a perfect finish, the découpage should be coated at least three times, with four hours drying time in between. From start to finish, a decorated item will take about a week to complete, but Caroline will often have 30 pieces on the go at any one time.

Recently, Caroline undertook a commission from a choir member of a production of Elgar's Dream of Geronitas, as a gift to the conductor. A beautiful waste paper basket was created, featuring music sheets from the piece and portraits of Elgar. The client was utterly delighted with the result, and the conductor was profoundly moved by such a personal gift. **PB**

When Louis Rich started his business it was based opposite the blacksmith at the rear of the Percy Bass building. As his business expanded, Louis took over the blacksmith's part of the building as well. Louis worked closely with Percy Bass himself and, despite being separate companies, the businesses still maintain an intimate relationship today.

In due course, Louis's two sons, Kenneth and Lawrence, both joined the company and it became Rich Brothers. Ten years ago, Danny Green joined Rich Brothers.

Virtually anything can be rebuilt to look as good as new

RESTORATION

RICH BROTHERS

When Kenneth and Lawrence Rich retired a few years ago, Danny took over the running of the business. He was assisted by Franco Bertagnin (now retired), who had worked for the Rich Brothers for 25 years, and Darren Pull. All three of these men possess exceptional skills in almost every aspect of restoration.

The workshop now specialises in antique restoration, furniture decoration, painting and gilding, chinoiserie restoration, marquetry repairs, replacing keys for drawers and boxes, inlay brass work, chandelier reconstruction, ceramics, lacquer work, and re-caning. Rich Borthers can also convert jars to lamps, carve wood and French polish. In fact, they can rebuild virtually anything to make it look as good as new. Conversely, the workshop can also 'antique' objects, giving them the appearance of age.

RESTORED TO ITS FORMER GLORY
Some restoration projects can take weeks to complete. A typical example is the renovation of an eighteenth-century chinoiserie mirror.

When it arrived in the workshop, it was in hundreds of different bits and pieces. The first job was to reassemble the whole mirror, strengthen it, and then make new pieces to replace the missing parts. The replacement pieces have to be modelled, hand-carved and then painted with a coat of gesso. The original glass in the mirror was useable, but it had to be re-silvered. Next, the mirror received a bole undercoat (made from extra-fine ground earth). This process is called 'assiette à dorer'. A yellow layer is applied, then red, followed by gold leaf (which comes in a book of wafer-thin pieces). This process is highly skilled and time consuming. The gilding is then burnished and splashed with a toner that dries to a powdery finish. When the excess powder is wiped away, the finished effect has more depth, which gives an 'aged' look to the mirror without detracting from its brightness. The completed mirror looked as magnificent as it would have done some 250 years earlier.

Lacquer work is a highly specialised process

Top right: Kenneth Rich.
Below right: Louis Rich.

Far right: An original door sign from the 1930s.

Lacquer work is also a highly specialised process. For example, the first base coat for oriental red lacquer is bright orange. The craftsman then has to paint a free-hand decoration onto the piece, and finally tones and polishes the object to produce the desired shiny red hue.

White china pots can be turned into chinoiserie vases. This is achieved by painting the item several times to make it less porous, then applying a fine ivory toning. After about five coats, designs are hand-painted onto the pots, which are then toned, polished and waxed. Black pots get a different treatment. They are painted black, then red and black again, before being polished and decorated appropriately.

INTRICATE DETAILS
Once chair frames have been repaired at Rich Brothers, they are then sent to Candido de Silva, who handles

Hit-the-rich

L. RICH,

DECORATIVE ARTIST.

13. CRESCENT PLACE, S.W.3.

ENGLAND

Evening Standard

The relationship between Percy Bass and the Rich brothers is almost unique among decorators

re-upholstery for Percy Bass. Danny likes to match furniture, and can seamlessly add replicas to a set of original dining chairs. Some of the restoration work at Rich Brothers is performed on a very small scale. Jewellery boxes often come in for repair, needing new silver, ivory or tortoiseshell inlays. Sometimes these boxes simply need to have their locks and keys replaced.

The materials used in the restoration process are not difficult to come by. They are all sourced from English suppliers, some of whom have been dealing with Rich Brothers for many years.

With so many different pieces passing through the workshop, there are inevitably some wacky items. Currently, a bizarre candle lamp is in for repair. The base consists of four real horses hooves, mounted in silver plate, with each hoof depicting a race meeting. One inscription reads '4th in the Grand National, 1897', and another 'Great Sefton Steeplechase, 1892'.

The relationship between Percy Bass and the Rich Brothers is virtually unique amongst decorators. With the consummate skills of Danny and Darren at the helm, Percy Bass can impeccably restore or duplicate almost any piece of furniture or decorative item that a customer chooses to present them with. **PB**

Above: The restored cabinet in situ.

Above left: Danny Green of Rich Brothers restoring an antique Chinese lacquer cabinet.

Opposite: One of many aspects of the Rich Brothers' business is French polishing.

If a project involves anything to do with paint, Maecenas can take it on

SCAGLIOLA
MAECENAS LTD.

There is nothing more exhilarating or inspiring for a decorator than to have a client with a wild imagination. If an unusual project involves anything to do with paint, then Maecenas can take it on – the only restrictions being practicality and, of course, budget.

Whether you would like a famous painting copied, your walls covered in hand-painted paper or gilded glass panels, this company has the relevant expertise to accommodate your request. The business is run by François Lavenir, who began his artistic career at the age of 15, painting a house as a summer job. There, he met an Italian master craftsman with the nickname, 'Titian'. When the summer job was complete, François went to work with Titian. He learnt a great deal, and has built on these skills with subsequent experimentation.

Some 20 years ago, François set up his business in the Crescent Place section of the Percy Bass building, where his skills were available to Percy Bass clients. Maecenas has since grown, and there are now up to 18 artists working in its current premises. Painting is a time-consuming process and there are always looming delivery dates to consider, so Maecenas often has several people working on a single project.

Above: Scagliola designs for table tops.

Opposite: Brushes in the Maecenas studio.

An intricate design for a table top made in scagliola. Note the detail in the rope border design.

Scagliola is the craft of imitating marble to recreate Florentine mosaic work

If a customer needs a copy of some antique wallpaper, it will usually be painted on lining paper. But, depending on the pattern, wide watercolour paper can also be used. Recently, the company made a copy of the wallpaper in Napoleon's bathroom at Rambouillet in France for a private house in California. The design was laid out on pieces of paper and then taken to Los Angeles. If one person had been working on the project, it would have taken 18 weeks to paint the panels by hand. Although the pattern was sourced from photographic references, it also had to be adapted to the particular shape of the Californian bathroom.

ACCURATE REPLICAS

When copying a wallpaper pattern, Maecenas begins by preparing the paper with two coats of primer, and then adds the pattern using a mixture of stencilling and freehand drawing. Some designs are requested more than once, such as the tree wallpaper found in the Swedish court theatre at Drottningholm. Other clients like to use a standard manufactured paper, and ask François to create a hand-painted border. For a more exclusive finish, wall coverings can be created to resemble fine marquetry or, for a truly stylish look, embossed leather is used to great effect in rooms such as libraries and studies.

The process for the creation of an embossed leather wall begins with the formation of an embossed mould, which is then made into a plaster cast. The mould goes to a factory to be cast in aluminium or bronze. This metal stamp is used to emboss the leather on a huge, sheeted press. When the leather has been stamped with the chosen design, it is returned to Maecenas for painting.

The company's artists have also painted ceilings. Projects have included a baroque cherub scene for a fashion showroom and the complete restoration of a gilt ceiling for a National Trust house.

Murals can be painted onto canvas, but larger projects have to be carried out in situ. These commissions can be from any period – Medici to modern. When painted onto the wardrobe doors of a small dressing room, a mural can create a valuable feeling of space.

FACE VALUE

Classical oil paintings can be copied, with a client's face substituted for the original character. One client asked to feature in a series of Pre-Raphaelite paintings, and another substituted the faces of family and friends for the originals in a Hogarth scene. Most of these paintings are undertaken by Fiona Sutcliffe. Interior designers are especially fond of incorporating copies of paintings in their design schemes, so that they can use a picture that is exactly the right size for a room. The original frames can also be copied and decorated.

Rosettes for ceilings are given a trompe l'œil treatment, and are carefully painted to give an illusion of light and shade. Another paint style that is currently popular is marbling. This is particularly helpful if a designer needs to disguise cabinet doors in marble bathrooms, as the stone itself would be far too heavy for ordinary door use. Unsightly, vertical support beams can be enhanced with a marble effect finish to give the impression of a classical column.

The Maecenas workshop also specialises in the decorative art of scagliola. This is the craft of creating imitation marble from plaster, and is used to reproduce the Florentine mosaic work known as pietre dure. A hard, industrial plaster is used, which is then carved to form the background shape. Consequently, as in pietre dure, the marble veining continues

Left: A copy of Napoleon's bathroom, hand-painted for a private house in Los Angeles.

Pietre dure techniques originated in ancient Rome, and were then revived in Renaissance Italy

all the way through the plaster. It is impossible to achieve this effect with a painted copy. The plaster designs are then cut and put into place, ready to receive the artificial marble. This substance is a mixture of plaster and powdered pigment; three or four colours are mixed into the plaster until it has a consistency similar to plasticine. This mixture is rolled into balls to create swirls of colour, emulating the patterns of marble. The mix is then pushed into the holes in the background moulds, and sets like modelling clay. Because of its consistency, the plaster is much more pliable than marble and is also easier to cut, which allows for more intricate designs. The decorations are then sanded down with fine paper and are finished with diamond pads, which give a glossy sheen.

RENAISSANCE REVIVAL
Pietre dure techniques originated in ancient Rome, and were then revived in

Renaissance Italy. The Grand Ducal studio was founded in 1588, and tools similar to those used for cutting precious stones were used to inlay lapis lazuli, agate and jasper into marble boxes, vessels and urns. Some of these designs have been executed in the Mannerist style, with stones elaborately set in gold mounts. Italian marble craftsmen also employed these intricate skills at the Manufacture des Gobelins in Paris.

Scagliola plaster work also has a long history, having been developed in Roman times as a poor man's marble. From the sixteenth century onwards, the technique was used to embellish interior columns and pilasters. There are many examples of this craft in Baroque churches in Italy and southern Germany. It has also been used to decorate floors, but requires a considerable amount of maintenance.

In the eighteenth century, scagliola became fashionable as a decorative finish for table tops, especially those made in Florence. However, there are also fine examples of scagliola work at Syon House and Spencer House in England. It is possible that English gentlemen on the Grand Tour would have seen these decorations in Italy and, upon their return, decided to add the effect to their own homes.

ART OF GLASS
The most popular trend in decorative art at the moment is for painted and gilded glass. This is often known as églomisé, or verre églomisé.

The term originates from a French art dealer called Jean-Baptiste Glomy, who died in 1786. He was known for his black and gold, etched glass frames for prints.

Scagliola has a long history ; This table top has a Florentine design.

Gold-engraved glass was first mentioned by Cellini in his manuscript *Il libro dell'arte*, written in the fourteenth century. Today, the pattern is etched onto the underside of the glass (sometimes with the aid of stencils) and all the edges are finished by hand. Gold is then applied, using either oil or water gilding techniques. A coat of coloured pigment (usually black) allows the design to stand out from its metal background. Early examples of églomisé depict both biblical and secular scenes. From the fifteenth century onwards, colour was added to the glass, reflecting the advance in the range of oil paints.

In late seventeenth- and early eighteenth-century England, églomisé was popular as a border for large mirrors, often featuring arabesque patterns. Later in the century, the technique was used by silhouettists and as a decoration for buttons on military uniforms.

The most popular decorative trend at the moment is for painted and gilded glass

Églomisé does not have to be used for traditional items – it is perfectly adaptable to modern use. Recent commissions have included a swirl design for a ceiling, made with real silver crushed into a resin. Other projects have involved a crushed foil decoration for a bedroom wall and panels for wall sconces, as well as entire pieces of furniture.

The Maecenas workshop thrives on the variety of its assignments, and has firmly established itself as a valuable centre of expertise for hand painting in any form. **PB**

Custom-made table and high chairs by Carew Jones. The chairs alternate in hot pink and chocolate brown suede.

Opposite: A Carew Jones contemporary display bookcase.

The company bases its reputation on the quality of its products and is now a market leader

Since 1989, the Carew Jones custom furniture business has occupied the main ground floor factory space in the Percy Bass building, with 188 Walton Street as its showroom entrance. From this location, Nigel Carew Jones established an innovative furniture business, which is now a market leader in modern British furniture design. The company bases its reputation on the quality of its products, and supports the British furniture industry by commissioning specialist workshops around the country to manufacture its designs.

CUSTOM FURNITURE

CAREW JONES

Though the company is now based in Chelsea, Carew Jones is the primary supplier of high-quality contemporary furniture for Percy Bass. Carew Jones furniture can be ordered in any size and is delivered in six to eight weeks (if selected from the current design range). However, about 40 per cent of the company's orders are for custom-made furniture. Nigel designs these pieces after detailed consultation with the client and the interior decorator.

CONTEMPORARY LOOKS IN TRADITIONAL SETTINGS
Nigel specialises in furniture made from Perspex, glass, lacquer, metal and timber (the latter including oak, sycamore, maple, Macassar ebony and American black walnut). The company also undertakes projects involving marquetry, contrast banding in ebony and 'book matched'

veneers. However, the company is best known for using man-made materials to create beautiful, high-quality, long-lasting furniture. This furniture is undoubtedly contemporary, but also looks stunning when placed in a traditional setting. Perspex is now completely accepted as a material for furniture production, as its simple lines enhance the beauty of classic interior design.

Perspex is now accepted as a durable material for furniture production

In 1969, Nigel first started work in the furniture department at one of the first Habitat stores, situated in Brompton Cross, at the end of Walton Street. In those days, the Habitat store was similar in style and quality to the current Conran Shop. It was an exciting time, as new materials were constantly coming to the market and were inevitably introduced to domestic interiors. Keen to expand his knowledge of furniture design, Nigel decided that he wanted to work for the furniture shop he most admired. He chose Albrizzi, run by Alessandro Albrizzi and Anthony Cloughley. They had just moved from the King's Road to a new showroom in Sloane Square, and specialised in exquisite, modern furniture. Nigel walked straight into the showroom and asked for a job. He quickly became the manager, then director and buyer, and was also responsible for exports to the company's showrooms in New York, Paris and Miami.

Below: A pair of art deco chairs sit comfortably with Carew Jones furniture in this room.

Later, Nigel left Albrizzi and spent the next five years running a furniture business in Belgravia (in partnership with interior designer Suzy Motley). Their client base initially consisted of most of the major City banks.

LACQUER POTENTIAL

In the early 1970s, Nigel was involved in the early development and design of high-gloss polyester lacquer in England. Working directly with pioneers of the lacquer workshops in the UK, he was instrumental in bringing the possibilities of this finish to the attention of the interior design world. The resulting finishes included metal inlays, faux crocodile, crackle and mottled effects, along with pearlised metallic surfaces.

Left: A stylish contemporary American oak and glass coffee table. Great attention has been paid to design detail.

A substantial amount of the company's stylish furniture is exported to the United States

Carew Jones has undertaken many lacquer projects, which have included fittings and furniture for luxury yachts and multi-coloured pianos for pop stars. A substantial amount of the company's stylish, contemporary furniture is exported to the United States, but it is also popular in Europe and, more recently, in Russia.

The use of Perspex as a medium for innovative furniture was beginning to evolve in the 1970s. During this decade, a client commissioned a Perspex table, which was then delivered in a minivan. As the driver passed over the Hammersmith flyover, the back doors flew open and the table shot out, landing on the carriageway below. He found the table in perfect condition, and continued with a successful delivery, proving the incredible durability of this furnishing material.

Carew Jones moved to 188 Walton Street in 1989. Initially, most of its customers were interior designers, but a small retail trade gradually developed. The company's relocation to the Percy Bass building meant that it could conveniently use the services of the other craftsmen based there (particularly Danny at Rich Brothers, for restoration, and Candido at Percy Bass for upholstery). He has also made table bases to accommodate scagliola table tops for François at Maecenas. The interior decorators at Percy Bass regularly commission furniture from Carew Jones, and Nigel often orders his fabrics from the extensive range of pattern books in the Percy Bass shop.

SMOKE AND MIRRORS

Nigel has recently had a lot of commissions for computer tables, often combining glass, Perspex and mirrors. He uses mirrored backs to hide unsightly cables. Carew Jones has recently developed a technique that invisibly bonds glass to glass. The company intends to fashion a range of glass furniture using this method of manufacture.

> Carew Jones has recently developed a technique that bonds glass to glass

Nigel was once asked by a Secretary of State to design a large meeting table for a political boardroom. A very small telephone table was placed alongside the meeting table. The system worked very well until a successor took office. Misunderstanding the original arrangement, the new incumbent assumed that the 2-foot-wide telephone table was his new desk, so Nigel received an irate telephone call from the department. When he arrived at the offices, Nigel found the 6 foot, 4 inch Secretary of State sitting in the middle of a very large room behind the tiny telephone table. A new desk was rapidly commissioned!

IN SITU

Nigel often visits project sites to see exactly where a piece of furniture is going to be placed, and he also likes to visit clients after delivery to see the end result. For more complex designs, Nigel often commissions scaled drawings from John Wilson at Percy Bass. The company regularly supplies furniture for boardrooms and conference centres. Nigel tends to team his tables with Boss chairs, covered in fine fabrics, leather or Ultrasuede.

Customers are becoming more confident about using contemporary furniture, so designers need an establishment where they can ask advice and see what manufacturers have to offer. Likewise, manufacturers need a place to display their latest products. Carew Jones fulfils both these roles by combining an eye for detail and quality with experience and cutting-edge design. **PB**

Above: Chairs from the Carew Jones range.

Left: A Digby writing/ dressing table.

Below far left: A Vernham lamp table in American oak and glass.

Bottom left: A Glebe cant cornered table in Perspex and glass.

Below right: A 'Rodenham' Perspex and glass coffee table.

Exquisite handmade passementerie: Left tassel, 'Lisboa'; right tassel, 'El Gordo' with pom poms; top fringe, 'Pendant'; centre fringe, S17P pom pom; bottom, G18 tassel; bottom left, 'Margot' cord tieback; bottom centre, cut ruche fringe; bottom right, bullion fringe.

PASSEMENTERIE
SMITH & BRIGHTY

Passementerie is the fine, decorative art of making tassels, fringes, ropes and tiebacks. It has a long history and is inextricably linked to the textile industry. During the eighteenth century, for instance, it was fashionable to have items made from gold or silver thread to match the cornice of a room and cast reflections in the soft, pre-electric light.

Marion Smith and Jane Brighty came into the passementerie business by chance. Both were diplomats' wives based in Lisbon when, one day, they passed a small shop displaying stunning fringes and tassels in the window. Sharing an interest in design and artisan skills, and deeply impressed by the quality of the work, the two women decided to visit the factory.

What they found was a building in a state of disrepair, with the upper floors

Items made from gold and silver thread were the height of eighteenth-century fashion

rented out as a retirement home. There were no samples, no names, no reference numbers and no price list. A large ledger, with hand-written descriptions of each product, served as the catalogue. But such was the beauty of the things produced there that Jane and Marion set about designing and ordering their own samples. Soon, they had their first six tassel tiebacks.

The tiebacks were exquisite and Marion and Jane felt sure there was a market for them. This marked the beginning of their education in the intricacies of passementerie, and of an

Above left: The trimmings on the Brunschwig & Fils linen cushions pulls this scheme together. The headboard is in Pierre Frey's Bengali, the butterfly cushion in the foreground is in 'Papillon' by Pierre Frey and the throw by de Le Cuoña.

Above right: A custom fringe being made on a hand loom in Smith & Brighty's Portuguese factory.

Above: The fringe on the cushions coordinates with the tassel tiebacks, pulling together the room's cream and pastel blue colours from a range from the Percy Bass shop.

Opposite: The fringe on the swags and tails of the curtains match a longer fringe on the sofa. The central cushion is fringed to complete the theme.

abiding fascination in, and passion for, the exquisite final product.

Jane took the samples to London and one of her first stops was Percy Bass. Everyone who saw the samples was impressed. Potential customers were particularly pleased when she explained that they could have any trimming custom-made to match any fabric in any colour. In fact, they could hardly believe it.

The original company was a small, friendly affair that supplied the local market

All of this happened in 1985 when handsome custom passementerie was difficult to find. Smith & Brighty received a few orders and the business grew from there.

Historically, the French were the masters of the industry. Their products were excellent, but exceedingly expensive. Marion and Jane felt that a more robust, more English/Portuguese style with a more accessible price could have a place in the market. So they began to develop an appropriate design ethos and style – one that has come to typify their product.

AN INTRICATE CRAFT

The original Portuguese company that Jane and Marion discovered was established in the 1930s. It was a small, friendly business supplying the local Portuguese market. Over the years, its workforce dwindled from 32 to ten, and after the revolution in 1974, business slumped. By 1986, the then owner, Senhor Sebastião, was considering other career options.

When Marion and Jane arrived, they persuaded Senhor Sebastião that there was a market for the right product in London. Marion, who was about to move to Washington DC, also convinced him that the United States could prove another profitable export market. Their plans went ahead, but with both Marion and Jane living outside Portugal, factory deliveries became erratic. Drastic action was necessary and the two English women concluded that the best option was to buy the factory.

Today, only about 20 per cent of the factory's output is for the domestic market. The remainder is exported, mainly to the United States and UK. A highly skilled workforce of 23 produces all items by hand, or on the original Jacquard or hand-looms, under the watchful eye of the manager, Senhor Americo Diaz, and the production manager, Dona Leonor.

Inset: The fringe on the curtain at picture rail height finishes the curtains in this bay window. The curtains are in Bennison's Rose Vine. Matching Rose Vine and striped cushions are by Bennison, and the foreground cushion is by Scalamandre in Medici's menagerie.

Tassel-making begins with shaped wooden balls made from elder wood in the traditional way

personal, with pieces of the weavers' work draped over them and the straps of the harness usually woven by the weaver himself.

The big, old Jacquard loom is used for making braid. It is really an early form of hand-cranked computer. For every design, a card must be punched. Then the loom has to be threaded up so that all the threads are laid down in the correct lines. This usually takes several days.

The machine has between eight and 12 'gates'. For maximum efficiency, it is best to produce different braids in each gate and run them all through at the same time. For long continuous runs, it is better to warp up several gates with the same design. All these processes require a particular skill and enormous patience.

Although the Jacquard loom is electrified, threads can snag or break at any time. Whenever this happens, the weaver has to rewind the threads meticulously, check for defects and then restart the machine. Fortunately, quality control seems to come naturally to the Portuguese workers.

The process of tassel-making is equally intricate. It begins with shaped wooden forms called 'balls', which are still made from elder wood in the traditional way. Some European manufacturers now use resin shapes, but Portuguese workers prefer the feel and weight of the original material.

The factory has a huge stock of viscose, wool, silk and cotton threads that have been dyed to every colour imaginable. An apprentice will take the required colour threads from the shelves and wind them up to appropriate thicknesses for weaving. The weaver will then prepare his own shuttles and bobbins to achieve the right tension. Fringes up to 13cm in height can be machine woven. Anything over 13cm is woven on the handloom. It can take up to a day to produce 9m of a complex fringe.

The machinery used at the factory is old and traditional, but can be mended easily. Often, all it takes is a little oil carefully applied by the operator. Most of the handlooms are made by the weavers themselves to a simple, sturdy design almost identical to the illustrations in Diderot's eighteenth-century encyclopaedia. They are very

A number of these wooden balls can be used together to form the body of the tassel (usually between two and five). Though there is a stock range, custom wooden shapes are regularly requested. A recent case was Windsor Castle, where Smith & Brighty were involved in making trimmings for the refurbishment after the disastrous fire. **PB**

Many of the great
furniture designers
past and present
have used horsehair
to great effect

TEXTILES
JOHN BOYD

In the picturesque rural landscape of northeast Somerset lies the pretty market town of Castle Cary. It is here that John Boyd, a textile merchant from Scotland, began his horsehair weaving business in 1837.

The town's history of weaving dates back to 1327 and the manufacture of a coarse, hard woven cloth known as Cary cloth (like calico). Then came mattress ticking, sailcloth and rope – all of which were made from the locally grown flax. Until the late eighteenth century, most people in the town were employed in agriculture or the wool industry – and with their decline, dramatic changes occurred in the social and economic fortunes of the town.

In the west country, where fashions were not followed with much speed, people were slow to grasp the economic consequences of imported linen. The result was a rapid decline in the wool trade, which left a gap in the marketplace and a ready-made workforce eager for alternative employment. In stepped John Boyd.

Boyd was an Ayrshire man who had been sent by his family to the neighbouring Somerset town of Wincanton, the national centre of linen manufacture. Wincanton had a history of attracting Scots involved in the drapery trade and Boyd was no different, working as a travelling drapery salesman for several years. With him was his friend and fellow Scot, William MacMillan, whose son William Wallace later became managing director of John Boyd Textiles.

John Boyd's business often took him to Castle Cary, where he observed a fledgling horsehair cottage industry growing in the town. A canny 22-year-old

Opposite: Horsehair fabric is traditionally used for dining chairs and suits a modern setting.

Left: The Gustavian dining table has matching chairs covered in black/brown horsehair fabric. This creates a striking contrast with the picture and Chinese black furniture. The wall paint is Farrow & Ball's Dix Blue.

Tails must be boiled for three hours in the dyeing room to make them colour-fast

with entrepreneurial tendencies, he immediately saw the commercial possibilities of horsehair weaving and set up in his own cottage in South Street. The original building can be seen there to this day.

Before Boyd arrived and gave the industry some much needed direction, horsehair weaving was a painstakingly slow, small-scale process; it took a month to produce and sell a piece of cloth just 50 yards long. First, the weaver went to market to buy the hair. Then, he would return home to weave the cloth. Finally, he went again to market to sell the cloth and buy more hair to start the process all over again. Smaller pieces of horsehair were sold off to make boot brushes, tooth and hairbrushes, wigs, sieve bottoms, cider cloths, hats, and plumes for soldiers' helmets. Nothing was wasted – even the pieces of hair that could not be used for weaving or utensils were collected and curled for stuffing chairs and mattresses.

The width of horsehair fabric is much narrower than other cloths because it can only be as wide as the length of a horse's tail. For black or grey hair, this is approximately 26 inches; for white, it is 22 inches. There was plenty of scope for getting hold of horsehair in Boyd's time because horses were working animals. Not only was it the fashion to crop the

tails, it was also a necessity: if left, they would often get mangled in the ploughs and farm machinery. Nowadays, the hair, which is always from live horses, comes from the Far East, where horses are still used to work the land.

By 1851, John Boyd's business had expanded to the employment of 30 women, 34 children and nine men, most of whom worked on looms at home. During this year, the business moved to a purpose-built factory. The children were taken on to pass the hairs individually to the weaver, but the Education Act of 1870 put an end to this practice. As it was uneconomic to employ adults for the task, Boyd invented a mechanical hair 'picker' that was attached to the latest mechanical looms. In 1872, Queen Victoria herself patented the picker.

Left and below: Horsehair fabric can be embroidered, adding another dimension to the range.

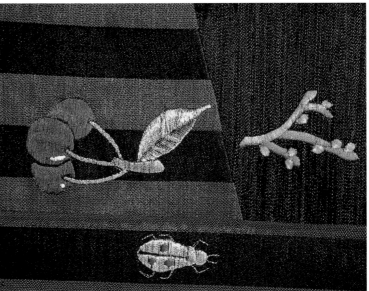

SURVIVING THE CENTURY

The looms made in Cary and Bruton at that time are the ones still used today in the only surviving horsehair textile weavers in the world. In fact, the Victorian period was a particularly successful time for the business. The colour palette was surprisingly bold, including a bright purple that they would only just have had the technology to produce. Until the death of Prince Albert, such colours were often chosen for dining room chairs. Afterwards, black, natural and

other 'gloomy' colours were favoured. Many of the designs from that era still enjoy popularity today.

Although John Boyd was a successful Victorian businessman, he had simple tastes and lived a modest life. He was a greatly respected benefactor and was very kind to his large workforce. In later life, Boyd built Jubilee Cottages in Cary – so named to celebrate the golden jubilee of Queen Victoria in 1887 – for the elderly poor. He also set up a fund that could be used to pay

the workforce when they were sick, but it was never needed. His employees were loyal and were one reason why the business survived harsh times.

Just before his death in 1890, Boyd made the business into a limited company. The new managing director was friend William MacMillan, natural history enthusiast and father to eight children. Sadly, several of the children died of cancer. One surviving child, Douglas, was responsible for starting the much-respected MacMillan Nurses charity.

The arrival of the twentieth century brought with it a few dips in the fortunes of the company, not all of which were related to Edwardian domestic fashions. During the First World War, the Boyd factory diversified to make tailors' padding cloth for officers' uniforms and military caps. By 1918, however, this cloth, which had kept 100 looms in operation, was no longer needed. Other difficulties ensued. First, a new material was being used for stuffing furniture. Second, the rise of motor transport brought about the demise of animal labour and therefore local horsehair. A new outlet in horsehair trade had opened in Russia (though this market quickly closed down with the Bolshevik

factory that it moved to in 1956. Originally, the looms' drive shaft was powered by a water mill and, for a short while, steam. Now, an electric motor provides the power, with the machines producing between two and three metres a day each from four horse tails. The tails are soaked for suppleness and fed into the warp one hair at a time by the 'picker' device.

Managing director Anna Smith (only the sixth in the company's 165-year history) has managed to keep ahead of fashion by introducing new colours, patterns and ideas. In fact, Boyd's fabric is among the world's finest quality niche fabrics, with 80–85 per cent of the product available for export. The

Opposite: Horsehair fabric blends perfectly into a contemporary setting.

Left: Example of embroided horse hair fabric in vibrant colours.

uprising in 1917) and, as if this was not enough, a crash in the US stock market followed. Boyd's kept afloat by streamlining the business, making economies and keeping hold of its highly skilled, determined employees, many of whom had been at the factory all their working lives.

In spite of the changing commercial landscape and the ready availability of synthetic fibres, the company continues to thrive. It is based at Higher Flax Mills, the former rope

company's largest market is Germany, where tight upholstery and a more formal style of furniture – Biedermeier, for instance – is popular. The second biggest market is the UK (one of the London outlets is Percy Bass), followed by the United States, which no longer has its own horsehair weaving industry.

Horsehair is durable and practical; it does not fade, stain or absorb food smells. Traditionally, it has been used for dining and library chairs, but is suitable for all close upholstery,

walling and lampshades. It is especially suited to the Empire styles, but is versatile and looks lustrous on modern furniture.

Many of the great furniture designers – Thomas Chippendale, George Hepplewhite, Sir Edwin Lutyens and Charles Rennie Mackintosh among them – have used horsehair. Mackintosh used a woven horsehair to cover the chairs at the Argyle Street tea rooms in Glasgow. When John Boyd Textiles was asked to reproduce the fabric, it took three years

brown in it), natural coloured hair is used for colours and mixed grey hair for strié. Natural white hair is rare and the most expensive, so is usually kept for violin bows.

Since horsehair is finer at the ends, two tails have to be matched end-to-stump to get an even distribution. Once this process is complete, the hair is ready for weaving. Hair can be woven in three different qualities: repp (coloured cotton warp, the same on both sides); sateen (horsehair

to perfect it. The reason was that the original was hand woven in Scotland with two different colours of hair, a process the mechanical looms found hard to match.

AN EXCLUSIVE OPTION

When horsehair arrives at the Boyd factory it is either black, mixed grey or natural white. It then goes through the processes of hackling, scouring, dyeing and conditioning until it is ready for weaving. In the dyeing room, the tails are laid out on trays and boiled for three hours to make them colour fast. Black hair is dyed black (natural black always has some dark

Embroidering adds another dimension to the product

showing mostly on one side); and damask (with an added woven pattern). It is then wrapped in a concertina fashion between boards and placed in an old cider press to be flattened.

A finer yarn is used if the finished cloth is to be embroidered. Embroidering adds another dimension to the product and is a custom service. Orders have included embroidered bees, cherries and coats of arms. Surprisingly though, among the colour and pattern choices on offer, the black Victorian weave with original code number '603' is still a bestseller. It is now called 'Holstein' after the breed of horse.

Among the most prestigious of Boyd's commissions are a sateen cloth for the decorative panels in the Royal Opera House in Stockholm and a damask for covering the chairs in the Royal Palace at Oslo. The architect Alva Aalto also saw the advantages of horsehair when he designed the Finlandia concert hall in Helsinki, and there is a Boyd fabric at the White House in Washington DC.

So if your chairs need recovering, horsehair fabric is an exclusive option. You could even pick up a stylish, glossy designer horsehair handbag to match. **PB**

Opposite: Charles Rennie Mackintosh used horsehair, fabric-covered chairs for the Argyle Street tea rooms in Glasgow. This Mackintosh chair has a frame in dark-stained sycamore.

Opposite, inset: The Napoleon chair was designed by Sir Edwin Lutyens. He often used horsehair fabric for his designs.

Left: A dining room chair, covered in horsehair and embroidered with feathers for an individual look.

Pugin's preference for gothic and natural forms
predominates throughout the Parliament buildings

At the top of Cole & Son notepaper, under the royal coat of arms, there is a statement that reads: 'by appointment to Her Majesty the Queen, suppliers of wallpaper, Cole & Son (Wallpapers) Ltd, manufacturers of hand printed wallpapers since 1875'. Although this projects the image of a company that is both established and establishment, the reality is that the future of Cole & Son has only recently been assured.

After a period of instability that left it close to permanent loss, the company re-established itself – under its original name – in October 2000. In June 2001, Cole & Son moved into a new, modern factory and re-employed its former workforce. Anthony Evans, the enthusiastic managing director, now runs a sound, forward-looking business that boasts a dynamic young team with innovative ideas. But the company can never be detached from its remarkable history. Indeed, it uses machinery dating back to 1902 and owns a precious archive of 3767 hand-carved wood blocks, some of which are 250 years old.

ART IN ISLINGTON

Wallpaper was first developed to simulate fine textiles. In England, it began to appear as small printed sheets, probably in a damask, around

Above and left: Double flock wallpaper in Committee Room 10, the Houses of Parliament.

WALLPAPERS
COLE & SON

the early sixteenth century. By the end of the seventeenth century, the technology had progressed enough to produce sheets of thick paper that could reach the height of a room. These would have been carefully pasted together to look like woollen hangings. Alternatives were leather from Spain and flock wallpapers from Holland, which were developed in 1685 and made to resemble fine Flemish tapestries.

Cole & Son was formed in the artisan area of Islington, North London in 1873 by John Perry. He became interested in the production and design of wallpaper by mixing with the artists and designers of the area. Together with a wallpaper designer called John Hanson, he produced a pattern book of eight designs, which is still in existence. All of the designs are hand-block printed and would have involved immense skill. They resemble the work of Christopher Dresser and had a colour palette limited to one or two shades. Customers would mostly have been architects.

The Perry-Hanson partnership, however, was not to last. Perry decided to continue the business on his own, moving into a purpose-built factory at the end of his garden in 1885. The factory was called the Offord Road works and the company remained there until the end of the twentieth century.

It was in this factory that Perry and his colleague Joseph Mason built various machines and used techniques that are still applied today. The business went from strength to strength. Perry invented a method of simulating silk by using mica (a mined mineral), discovered a way of

creating a moiré (watermark effect) on paper and developed another medium called jaspé. The latter is a strié (brushed effect) that Perry discovered after watching silk being dyed in France and emulating the look on paper. Significantly, he revived the art of flocking wallpapers to look like embossed velvet. Indeed, it is these double flock hand-blocked papers that are so admired today. Later, other techniques were added to the repertoire, including graining and marbling on paper, leather embossing and gauffrage (embossed velvet).

Eventually, this busy business expanded its customer base to include large trade houses, like Harrods. It even drew the attention of Buckingham Palace, where Perry's papers were hung in George V and Queen Mary's apartments. Although Perry had no retail outlet, he produced special grounds and block printing to customers' requirements. Some blocks had up to 16 colours and the designs included dado, friezes, borders, and panoramas with bird and butterfly motifs. As rival manufacturers were forced out of business, Perry bought their wood printing blocks, building up a large collection over the years. One acquisition was for the blocks from H. Scott Richmond whose designs included work by H.H. Mott (who designed for G.F. Bodley at Watts & Co.).

THE BIRTH OF COLE & SON

Among John Perry's customers was Albert Cole, a successful wallpaper merchant and owner of Cole & Son, Wallpapers Ltd. (established in 1934). Albert had begun his career at a wallpaper and paint company called Knowles & Co. on the King's Road in Chelsea. He then joined a colleague, Lionel Hill, to form Cole & Hill in 1910. The business, based at Berners Street in the West End, was a complete decorators' merchant for top-of-the-trade products, including hand-printed wallpapers from Zuber in France, Morris & Co., Jeffrey & Co. – and John Perry.

When Perry died in 1940, the family put the business up for sale. Albert Cole decided to take a risk in difficult wartime conditions and purchased it. He also took on all the staff and the wooden printing blocks. But it didn't stop there. Cole busily bought other printing blocks, such as the historic collection of Cowtan & Son (who also held the work of J.C. Crace & Son). This was a hugely important purchase that provided Cole with an archive spanning five generations and two centuries.

The Crace family had furnished many palaces, castles and stately homes. They carried out work for Henry Holland on Brighton Pavilion and for George IV at Windsor Castle. It was John Gregory Crace who had taken all the interior decorating orders and designs from Augustus Pugin, the gothic designer famous for his prolificacy and the wallpapers at the Houses of Parliament.

Pugin had taken forward reforms of mid-nineteenth century wallpaper designs, which had become over-busy with loud colouration and brash floral motifs. He thought wallpaper design should be two-dimensional and rely on authentic historical sources. Following this belief and imposing his principles of gothic and natural forms, Pugin produced over 100 designs for the Houses of Parliament. Crace was entrusted with selecting the colours for them, adding details of heraldic emblems and devices, and cutting and printing the blocks. Printing was contracted out to Scott, Cuthbertson & Co. (When this company went out of business, Cole purchased the remaining blocks for the public areas in the Palace of Westminster. The private apartments' blocks went to Watts & Co.)

The acquisition of the Perry and Cowtan archives added to Albert Cole's own range and put him in possession of the largest wood block collection in the trade (dating back to 1750). Immediately, he began to print some of the most interesting designs, including Fuschia and the Humming Birds. The

Opposite: Flat-printed wallpaper by Pugin, used in the Little Parlour at Strawberry Hill.

Below: The eighteenth-century home of Horace Walpole, Strawberry Hill, Twickenham.

Between them, the Cole's employees had nearly 600 years of experience in their specialised crafts

latter dates from 1770 and has recently been relaunched by Cole & Son in four colourways with a matching fabric.

AN ERA OF CHANGE

In 1995, Walker Greenbank purchased Cole & Son. Anthony Evans joined as managing director, having spent the previous 13 years running his own wallpaper and textile shop in Knightsbridge. Shortly afterwards, the new owners decided to transfer the management and sales departments to another company in the group (Zoffany), making Evans redundant. Then, believing that the old Offord Road works was not cost effective, they moved the business to their Loughborough headquarters. When the workforce, who had lived in Islington all their lives, refused to follow they were also made redundant.

Between them, the Cole's employees had 500–600 years of experience in their specialised crafts. Walker Greenbank found itself unable to manufacture the same product and Cole & Son was, once again, up for sale. Anthony Evans sought to buy the company with Tim Burles and designer Karen Beauchamp. After some disappointing moments in the City, they were lucky enough to find a New York backer, Christopher Ohstrom, who owned a hand-blocked wallpaper business in the United States.

In 2001, after 126 years, the business moved from Offord Road to a modern factory in North London. All the original machines, the archive of wood blocks, John Perry's original desk and a re-hired workforce went with it. The Cole & Son showroom has also been through a few changes. It moved to Berners Street in 1934 and subsequently to Mortimer Street in the West End. It remained there until the end of the twentieth century and was run as a gentleman's business, with each employee receiving their own hand towel for the week on a Monday morning and the managing director lunching every day at Wheeler's restaurant. Recently, it moved to new premises in Chelsea Harbour.

HAND-BLOCKING, FLOCKING AND CRUSHING

Among the buildings that regularly require customised wallpaper are Balmoral Castle, Buckingham Palace, The White House and Woburn Abbey. In fact, the list of landmark properties is endless. Not all of the Cole's business is bespoke, however. Many of the designs are appropriate for general domestic use. Handmade stripes of varying widths come in 80 colours, and a soft diaper, patterned paper called Clandon is a best seller in the stock books (and has been since 1920). Other collections include Salisbury, Barnsbury, Buckingham and Dennis Hall.

Wallpaper-making is a lengthy process and involves numerous handlings. Quality-weight lignum paper is ideal because of its strength. Another advantage is that it doesn't yellow with age because all the wood has been removed from it. Stock papers can be produced relatively quickly using the same processes that Perry did all those years ago. Colours are mixed by eye

from distemper, a water-soluble and chemical-free mix of chalk and casein that can be easily rinsed off the blocks, then printed into the paper (dye-coated). Finally, a glaze is applied by a glazing machine that dates back to 1926.

Hand-block printing begins with a block dipped into a tray of colour. It is then stamped on to pre-trimmed, pre-aligned paper and pulses of pressure are applied. The process is repeated until a whole strip is complete. That strip is festooned on hangers to dry, with wooden clothes pegs keeping it securely in place. Only a very highly skilled workforce can perform this process. At Cole's, there is a long apprenticeship, but no retirement age. Some employees have been at the company for 50 years and there is a great team spirit.

When customers request reprints of original Pugin designs, the highly specialist staff at Cole's often have to perform flocking. Flocking is a very labour intensive process – it takes three men (one with 38 years'

Above: Rolls of wallpaper – past and present.

Opposite: A featureless sitting room is given character by using Cole's red Windsor stripe wallpaper. The stool is covered in Watts of Westminster's Shrewsbury, the pair of cushions by Ralph Lauren and heraldic cushion by Nina Campbell. The curtains are in Bennison's faded blue roses.

experience) ten days to make enough paper for a small order. The process begins when a block is dipped into a tray of molitice adhesive. The block is then stamped very carefully on to a length of paper (the design outline is touched up by hand). Next, the paper is slowly pulled along a trestle table and past a flocker, who sprinkles rayon fibres on by hand. A machine below the table beats the paper up and down to regulate the distribution of the flock. The final stage is when one of the workers hoists the paper on to the festoons to dry.

The antiquated machinery used at Cole & Son still produces a high-quality product. There is a late-1940s hand trimmer with strings and weights, a moiré machine and a gauffrage machine for embossing velvet. Many customers choose to send their velvet to Cole's, where it is crushed through three rollers. The first is heated, the second holds the pattern (usually of nineteenth-century origin) and the third applies the pressure. Since different types of velvet require different treatments and pressures, a high level of skill is required.

Cole & Son, part antiquated, part thriving commercial business, offers surface-printed vinyls and machine-printed wallpapers, as well as screen- and block-printed wallpapers and flock. It owes its survival to the enthusiasm and determination of Anthony Evans. This charming man, who strides around the factory wearing flamboyant I Zingari socks, is truly passionate about wallpaper. **PB**

The Gainsborough Silk Weaving Co. is situated in Sudbury, on the Suffolk/Essex border. It takes its name from the town's most famous resident, the eighteenth-century portrait artist, Thomas Gainsborough.

Reginald Warner, born in 1880, founded the company. His father, Metford Warner, was the proprietor of Jeffrey's & Co. (a workshop that produced outstandingly elegant block-printed wallpapers) and worked closely with designers such as William Morris (a friend), Owen Jones and Walter Crane. Reginald's brother Horace was a wallpaper designer at Jeffrey's and another brother, Marcus, was in charge of the firm's production area. Together with two sisters, the family lived in Highbury Park, North London, and were active members of the local Quaker community.

The Warner family were originally Huguenots. The Huguenots were widely persecuted in France and Belgium and, after the Revocation of the Edict of Nantes in 1685, expelled. Many were silk weavers. They and their families migrated to Spitalfields in the East End, where they soon found work. But the introduction of a minimum wage, which employers were not prepared to pay, pushed the weavers either eastwards to the Suffolk/Essex border or to Macclesfield in Cheshire. Both wool and cotton production in these areas was in decline, so the silk weaving business provided a welcome boost.

Opposite: An antique sofa covered in Gainsborough red silk damask. Curtain fabric and check roller blinds by Colefax & Fowler, floral cushions by Bennison and backgammon set by David Linley.

Below: Fabrics are woven in the traditional way.

SILKS
GAINSBOROUGH SILK WEAVING CO.

later, in 1904, he married Margaret Rose of the Rose's Lime Juice family in Felixstowe.

In the early days, Reginald designed and cut his own pattern cards. He also helped to develop a self-twiller mechanism that could be attached to the basic Jacquard machine, and pioneered a method of warp thread control that allowed punched holes to produce the required design. This combination of engineering, artistic and weaving skills translated into high-quality silk damasks, tapestries, and plain and figured velvets. A company highlight was when the Princess of Wales visited in 1906 and ordered silk damask for a Durbar Dress for a state visit to India.

The business expanded and, thanks to family connections, its products were increasingly sought after by leading interior decorators in London. In 1924, the business left behind its cottage industry origins and moved to the purpose-built weaving shed that is still its home. In those days, the building housed hand looms and hand-warping mills. It later became more self-sufficient by adding facilities to wind and dye the materials.

Opposite, above: A vibrant scheme for Wimborne House in Arlington Street, London by Gainsborough using red silk damask 156/8599 on the walls and for the festoon blinds.

Opposite, below: The chair is covered in a silk/cotton stock design S9547. The gold curtain is also a silk/cotton D21374.

Left: Dramatic gold/black fabric on this wing chair is a stock range silk/cotton chenille called Renaissance Damask D21373.

Huguenot families in the Essex area included Warner & Son, fabric manufacturers who wove at Halstead for 100 years, and the Courtauld family at Braintree. Today, Sudbury is the largest silk production town in Europe. Most of the production there is for the fashion industry and includes the making of scarves, ties and other apparel. Gainsborough is a small, but important part of this weaving community.

THE PATH OF PROGRESS

From the age of 13, Reginald Warner wanted to be a weaver. So as soon as he was old enough, he took an apprenticeship at The English Silk Weaving Company in Ipswich, a hand weaving business conveniently located near a Quaker friends meeting house. When this company fell into liquidation, the entrepreneurial Reginald set up The Gainsborough Silk Weaving Company. He was just 23. A year

Clients can choose from over 2000 historical reproductions

The 1930s heralded the arrival of power looms, but progress was curtailed when the company set aside its business to weave parachute silk and heavy blackout fabric for the war effort. After electrification in the 1950s, technology progressed slowly until the invention of the modern rapier looms and computerised, electronic Jacquard looms in the 1980s. Gainsborough survived all these changes and succession was assured when Reginald's son took over. The company is still run by direct descent and is now managed by the fourth generation.

RAW SILK TO RARE BEAUTY

Silk is imported mostly from China and still travels across the old 'Silk Road' until it reaches the Como region of northern Italy.

In Como, workers called 'throwsters' spin raw yarn into different thicknesses (deniers) of spun yarn. Agents in the UK, who would have organised the whole procedure, then purchase the spun yarn and have it shipped back home.

Supply and demand varies according to the harvest in China. Most farmers there have a small production of cocoons and send their wares to a cooperative for sale. Sometimes weavers can get raw material easily, at other times it is very difficult. Also, while the right quantity might be available, the quality of the silk may not be premium. Gainsborough only buys premium. Good-quality, single-filament silk yarn should feel slightly crunchy, like freshly-fallen snow.

Silk weaving itself is highly specialised and labour intensive. The first stage is dyeing. Silk takes very well to colours – particularly reds, yellows and blues. All the natural fibres are dyed in hanks as this produces a much more even colour than dyeing on large cones. The silk is then wound on to bobbins for conversion into warp and weft before being woven into the custom or stock design.

As a young man, Reginald Warner studied weaving in Switzerland and purchased a large collection of European woven textiles (mostly from liquidating French weaving companies). This collection formed the basis of the Gainsborough archive to which another 100 years of designs – from Medieval Gothic to Art Deco – has since been added. Clients can now choose from over 2000 historical reproductions in various colour ways, with the minimum order being 98 feet (30m).

There are 40 designs in the stock ranges with over 300 colourways. They vary from the Palace Collection, a classic 100 per cent silk damask, to Alexander (a cotton damask range) and Medici, a cotton viscose damask range that coordinates with a Smith & Brighty trimmings range. Interestingly, these two companies have forged a strong link as both offer the highest quality production skills.

SUPPLYING ROYALTY –
AND THE WORLD
Despite the company's name, only about 20 per cent of Gainsborough's output is silk. Most of the production is cotton, a silk and cotton mix (silk for the warp and cotton for the weft), and other natural fibre yarns like flax and wool. These fabrics can be used for upholstery, walling, cushions, lampshades, bedcovers, drapes and curtains. Damask walling is particularly popular for galleries (the National Gallery is one of Gainsborough's most high-profile clients).

Around 40 per cent of the company's production is custom-made and has been exported all over the world, mostly through interior designers. One recent commission was for a fabric with a 20-foot (6m) repeat

for a theatre in New York. The United States is actually Gainsborough's largest export market and where the company has chosen, for the first time, to launch its products under its own name. Decorative art centres across the country – including Washington, New York, Atlanta, Dallas, Phoenix, Los Angeles, Fort Lauderdale, San Francisco, Houston, Denver and San Diego – will soon be selling Gainsborough originals.

Expertise in historical reproduction has helped the Gainsborough Silk Weaving Company to establish a reputation for exquisite quality and attention to detail. This, in turn, has enabled it to carve out a niche in the interior design market as a specialist supplier. Commissions include historic fabrics for the National Trust (at Uppark, Chartwell, Hinton Ampney and Lyme Park); British Embassies; the House of Commons; The Admiralty; Spencer House and Marlborough House; Middle Eastern Embassies; The Sultan of Brunei; and the Royal Palaces of Bahrain, Sweden and Denmark.

Gainsborough has established a reputation for exquisite quality and attention to detail

Since 1985, Gainsborough has held a Royal Warrant for the manufacture of furnishing fabrics for The Queen. Among the commissions are supplying every British Royal household – from Balmoral and Buckingham Palace to Clarence House and Windsor Castle – with fabrics for furnishings and curtains. The company's current project is to supply fabrics for the stagecoaches at the Royal Mews.

Not all specially commissioned fabrics for the Royal Family have been for furnishings or curtain treatments, however. Before the Queen Mother's eightieth birthday, Princess Margaret asked Gainsborough to weave some Royal Stewart tartan material. The idea was that it could be made into sashes for members of the Royal Family, including the Queen Mother herself. **PB**

Opposite: Silk damask walls are a traditional backdrop for portraits. The blue is coordinated in the cushions and complements the colours in the carpet.

Opposite inset: A Regency stool covered in gold silk damask.

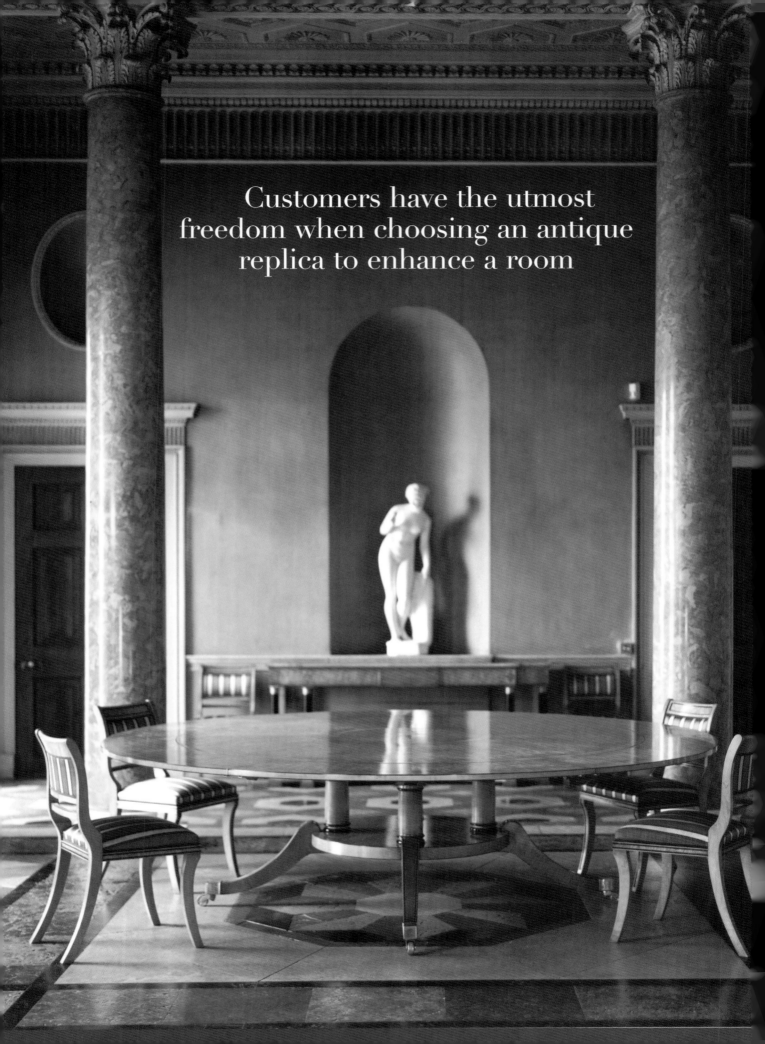

Customers have the utmost freedom when choosing an antique replica to enhance a room

I pswich in Suffolk has always been known for its wood business and craftsmen. Once a major shipbuilding area, its coat of arms shows a lion rampant bearing a galleon. This heraldic emblem is the company logo of Titchmarsh & Goodwin, cabinet makers of distinction. Currently run by brothers Jeremy and Peter Goodwin, the company was started in 1920 by their father Gordon and his brother-in-law, Lawrence Titchmarsh. Sadly, that partnership did not last more than a decade as Titchmarsh moved away to pursue sporting interests.

Although the company is only 80 years old, there has been a tradition of fine furniture making in the Goodwin family since 1770. At that time, Samuel Goodwin, a Suffolk carpenter, sent his son George to London to learn skills from one of the great cabinet makers of the day. This was normal practice and on George's return to Ipswich, he embarked on a career in furniture and clock-case making.

In 1925, Titchmarsh & Goodwin, which has always been based in Ipswich, moved into its present premises at Back Hamlet. It prospered right until the outbreak of the Second World War. A few years on, in 1959, a London showroom opened in Curzon Street, Mayfair, but a terrible setback was to follow. A fire ravaged the factory in 1963, destroying all the machinery. Thanks to the loyalty of the workforce and its customers, the company recovered from the disaster.

Today, the workforce numbers about 70 and consists of wood turners, carvers, cabinet makers, French polishers, a gilder, glazier and lacquer artist. Some craftsmen have been in their highly skilled posts for 30 or 40 years. But this is also a youthful team. Suffolk College is one of the best training grounds in England for woodwork, so finding new recruits is not a problem.

WORKING WITH WOOD

The backbone of Titchmarsh & Goodwin is, and always has been, its work in oak (which accounts for half of all output). Quality is second to none. Every detail is authentically reproduced from sixteenth- to nineteenth-century sources, including hinges, handles, escutcheons, locks and steel keys. Every piece is hand polished – in fact, it can take up to 18 separate processes to build the

Opposite: A dining table and chairs in Karelian birch – a popular light wood.

Below: Delivering a particularly large table.

CABINET MAKERS
TITCHMARSH & GOODWIN

patina to the required standard. It is this loving care that gives Titchmarsh & Goodwin its unrivalled reputation.

Another part of this family business is fine veneer work, a skill brought to England by Huguenot craftsmen in the mid-1650s. The company has carried on the traditions of Thomas Chippendale, George Hepplewhite, and Thomas Sheraton using walnut, mahogany, satinwood, rosewood and yew. Yew was popular after the Second World War because customers wanted something different, but walnut is especially prized for its beautiful texture, grain and colour.

It was the Romans who brought the European walnut tree to the British Isles, while the black walnut tree originates from the United States. Both varieties are highly sought after for fine cabinet work. In the eighteenth century, walnut was the preferred wood for furniture and was mostly imported from France. Then a disease struck the trees and export of walnut wood was banned. This is the main reason why tastes shifted to mahogany in the nineteenth century. At that time, mahogany could easily be obtained from the British West Indies (mainly Jamaica), but recent fashion has seen a decline in its use. The reason is partly to do with environmental concerns, and partly linked to the rising popularity of lighter coloured woods.

Titchmarsh & Goodwin customers have the utmost freedom when choosing an antique replica to enhance a room or add to a collection. Catalogues show thousands of designs in English hard woods, including ash, wild cherry, mulberry and laburnum. Sweet chestnut, a popular native of East Anglia, is rarely used however as it was tragically blighted by the great storm of October 1987. Stocks are low and expensive.

Recently, Peter Goodwin introduced Karelian birch to the range. Though it is a difficult wood to work with (it is brittle and tricky to polish), the company's skilled craftsmen can bring it to a beautiful finish. This pale, honey coloured burr veneer looks exquisite in designs highlighted with ebonised features and is proving very popular.

Karelian birch grows in a small region of eastern Finland called Karelia. Due to the landscape and unique soil conditions of that area, it produces an unusual but entirely natural burr figuration. The trees are harvested during winter as they can only be extracted when the ground is deeply frozen. Horses are used during this process.

Titchmarsh & Goodwin manages woodlands at Edwardstone in Suffolk and is developing its own tree nursery. The company also owns sawmills at the nearby village of Witnesham. Most of the timber used actually comes from mature woodlands in East Anglia, and is cut and air-dried in the traditional way. There have been some other unusual sources though. A few years ago, the owners of Holkham Hall in north Norfolk requested that a huge diseased elm be removed from the front of the mansion. It was subsequently made into many 14x5 foot-long tables with a beautiful grain.

THE ART OF ORIENTAL LACQUERING

One of the business's other specialities is oriental lacquer work, which is done by their resident artist and expert in the field, John Sadler. The process is complex and time consuming. First, John uses an animal glue to get rid of all the grain and produce a smooth surface. Next, he mixes the glue with different coloured chalks to stop the surface chipping. After applying two or three coats, he rubs the surface down and uses a mixture of three different oils to prepare for the application of background colour.

In other establishments, colour is often sprayed on, but John Sadler does it by hand for a finer quality finish. He uses three brushes and different colours to create a surface that is a darker shade towards the outside. This gives the illusion of shade and antiquity. When the surface is dry, John places a sheet of tracing paper on it that has a pin-pricked pattern and sprinkles chalk over the holes. The design has to be added in this way because drawing on the surface would leave holes or dents.

John's designs are never the same and cannot be easily copied because he does them all by hand. Usually, they include fretwork edges with mountains, oriental

buildings and figures. The raised pieces for the mountains and figures are made using a secret formula, and a powdered metal base is flicked on to produce a 'faded' gold, silver or bronze relief. There then follows a series of sealing, polishing and varnishing processes before the 'crack effect' varnish is applied. This varnish used to be mixed by hand, but now comes as a ready-prepared product. Application has to be done extremely carefully to create an even effect. Once the large lock plates and hinges have been fitted, the piece is finished. The results are always individual, stunning antiques of the future.

Titchmarsh & Goodwin exports about 20 per cent of its work and custom makes 10–15 per cent. Unsurprisingly, most of the royal houses in Europe have bought its furniture at some time over the last 40 years, together with governments and some of the world's biggest companies. Jeremy Goodwin remembers one commission for Algernon Asprey in the 1970s. The furniture was shipped to Kathmandu in Nepal in a Boeing 707. Its destination – the Royal Palace. **PB**

Above: Half of Titchmarch & Goodwin's commissions are for oak – authentically reproduced from traditional styles

Opposite above: The bulbous carved legs and wooden stretchers are authentic features for this Elizabethan style oak dining table and complement the oak panelled walls.

Opposite inset: A selection from thousands of wood templates, which all had to be replaced after the 1963 fire.

Opposite below: A drop-leaf oak table and dining chairs with rattan seats stylistically match the finely detailed oak dresser.

TEXTILES & WALLPAPERS
WATTS OF WESTMINSTER

I t is widely assumed that Watts are suppliers of ecclesiastical fabrics and Pugin wallpapers, and that the basis of the company is firmly Gothic. In fact, the majority of its archive is Queen Anne revival and for domestic use.

The founding partners of Watts & Co. were three distinguished architects: George Frederick Bodley, Thomas Garner and George Gilbert Scott Jnr. They set up the company in 1874 to provide furnishings, fixtures and interior design services for the architectural projects in which they were involved. All three were former pupils of Gilbert Scott's father, Sir George Gilbert Scott, the architect responsible for St. Pancras Station's Midland Hotel, The Foreign Office and The Albert Memorial.

Throughout the nineteenth century, architecture was considered a high art. Architects were expected to produce a total design concept – from the fixtures and fittings, to furniture and the building itself. They were also responsible for giving commissions to artists. Sir George Gilbert Scott built up a lucrative architectural practice with his partner W.D. Moffatt in the 1830s and 1840s. They began by building workhouses in a simple classical style, but soon moved on to cathedrals, churches, domestic dwellings and public monuments. In the end, some 18,000 buildings had input from Scott's practice, including remodelling and restoration projects.

Opposite: A sofa covered in 'Shrewsbury' sits comfortably in an authentically decorated Victorian room. The building was designed by Richard Norman Shaw.

Left: G.F. Bodley (standing) and George Gilbert Scott Jnr. (seated).

Sir George became a follower of Pugin and was a leading player in the Victorian Gothic revival. He had great energy and attracted first the renowned architect G.E. Street, then Bodley, Garner and George Gilbert Scott Jnr. to his practice. These last three, together with Street's pupils Philip Webb, William Morris and John Dando Sedding, were destined to become the leading lights of the next architectural generation.

CHURCH ART AND ARCHITECTS

Church building was prolific in the mid-nineteenth century. In 1859, Bodley began a church project in Brighton (St. Michael's) and gave William Morris's new company, Morris Marshall Faulkner & Co., its first commission for stained glass and painted decorative treatments. Morris saw the merits of setting up a decorative arts business to cope with the church building boom and went into partnership with Philip Webb, Edward Burne-Jones, Dante Gabriel Rossetti and Ford Madox Brown (among others). Further church interior commissions from Bodley followed at Selsley in Gloucestershire and St. Martin's-on-the-Cliff in Scarborough. St. Martin's-on-the-Cliff is a veritable treasure trove of Pre-Raphaelite art from Ford Madox Brown and Burne-Jones, stained glass by Rossetti, and an embroidered altar frontal designed by Morris himself.

embrace other ideals. Pugin, who championed the decorated gothic, and the philosopher John Ruskin were their main influences. Ruskin believed in honesty of purpose. A good building, he thought, was one that had been built by good craftsmen and expressed one's life. The Hogarth Club members also talked with, influenced and helped each other. Webb once checked on one of Bodley's building projects, and Bodley produced early wallpaper designs with Webb for Morris & Co. (as it was later called).

Over the years, Bodley's style changed to adopt medieval principles. It was a shift that led to clashes with his old collaborator William Morris, most notably when they were working on All Saints church in Jesus Lane, Cambridge. Bodley did not like the artistic licence with which Morris, who was actually moving away from this type of work, had created the

Queen Anne revival encompassed everything from red brick buildings to flat-patterned wallpapers

In 1869, Bodley set up an architectural practice with Thomas Garner. The two men shared the same sense of refinement: Bodley was a perfectionist (he produced 35 drawings for one block of stone) and Garner, whose focus was domestic buildings, loved harmony and texture. Both were members of the Hogarth Club, which Rossetti had set up as an alternative to the Royal Academy.

This entire generation of late Victorian architects and artists were rebels. They were ready to move away from the Victorian era obsessions with gloomy opulence, over-stuffed furniture and rooms cluttered with possessions, to

stained glass and colouring of the church. They parted company.

Of the six architects trained by Scott & Street, Morris and Sedding moved into the Arts and Crafts movement; Webb embraced both Arts and Crafts (Standen, West Sussex, 1892–94) and Queen Anne revival (Clouds, Wiltshire, 1879–91); and Bodley, Garner and Gilbert Scott Jnr. adopted the eclecticism of Queen Anne revival. This style encompassed everything from red brick buildings with tall chimneys, to sumptuous fabrics, lighter woods for furniture and brighter, flat-patterned wallpapers. Interior features included blue and white oriental and Delft porcelain, as

'Pear' hand-blocked wallpaper, c.1880, by G.F. Bodley; 'Drummond' curtains by Pugin, c.1850, in woven woollen stuff.

well as Persian carpets, eighteenth-century furniture and portraits.

Bodley and Garner started to produce their own decorative art and set up a company called Burlison & Grylis. Run by Garner, the company was responsible for some of the finest stained glass of the later nineteenth century. However, the founders struggled to find the wallpapers and decorative accessories they needed. Thinking that Morris & Co. was becoming old fashioned, they started a rival business in partnership with George Gilbert Scott Jnr. When it came to choosing a name for the new enterprise, the three decided on Watts, derived from 'What's in a name?' It seemed an ideal way to dissociate their names from trade.

CLIENTS, ROBES AND WALLPAPER

Watts & Co. started out in a showroom at Scott's practice on Duke Street, Portland Place. It then moved to the ultra-fashionable Baker Street. Suddenly, the three architects had the artistic freedom they wanted for both church and domestic projects. They advertised 'Wall Papers, Printed and Woven Stuffs for Wall Hangings', as well as other materials like church embroidery. They also sent out a prospectus confirming that they did metal work and made fire grates, door furniture and tiles. Examples of the projects the company undertook include the internal decoration of St. Augustine's Church, Kilburn, for architect J.L. Pearson; the conservation and refurbishment of Ham House; and Treasurer's House, York.

Watts & Co. served a totally different market to its competitor. Morris & Co. had a commercial business that allowed customers to come to the shop at Baker Street, walk around it and order from pattern books. Watts & Co. catered for a discerning, sophisticated clientele who ordered custom-made, opulent furnishings. Morris & Co. did not survive the downturn in business caused by the First World War, closing in 1923 (although its stock ranges and archives were put to commercial use later on). Watts & Co. survived both the war and the austere period that followed by concentrating on the ecclesiastical side of its output. Another factor was Bodley's fashionable status, which remained intact right until his death in 1907.

After its move to Dacre Street in 1952, Watts continued to make silverware, altar frontals, church hardware, stained glass and church embroidery. It also made vestments. Vicars and deans would order copes and stoles made in purple for Lent and Advent, green for Trinity and red, cream or gold for festive occasions like

Vicars and deans would order copes and stoles in a variety of colours

Easter, Christmas and Harvest Festival. Exquisite damasks, silks and patterned silks with heraldic emblems were available. Coronation robes were another of the company's specialities.

In 1960, Watts & Co. moved to its present location at Faith House, Tufton Street, in the environs of Westminster Abbey. Of course, it was still in possession of its archive of wallpapers, including the Pugin designs that were commissioned for the domestic apartments at the Houses of Parliament. (It had acquired these when the printers for Watts and Pugin wallpapers, Scott Cuthertson, went out of business.) The designs continued to sell, helped along by John Betjeman and Noel Coward who 'discovered' Watts and spread

Opposite left: Bamboo Jasmine Summer wallpaper, 1871–6, by G F Bodley is still popular today.

Opposite right, above: Chair is covered in D'Urberville summer ochre made up in a linen/cotton mixture.

Below: 'Malvern' in black taupe 'old gold' made in a Jacquard weave cotton silk.

the word in their literary circles. A change in fashion played a part in Watts' fortunes too. The Victorian Society was formed (with Watts & Co. the only advertiser in the first edition of their magazine); Osborne & Little started a resurgence of colour; and then Zoffany and Laura Ashley came along with their romantic vision of Victoriana.

NAMES AND PLACES

One of the greatest influences on Watts & Co. was the remarkable Elizabeth Hoare, the great granddaughter of Sir George Gilbert Scott. She inherited the business in 1953 and remained hands-on until her death in 2001. Elizabeth spent a great deal of time collecting nineteenth- and twentieth-century church embroidery. This magnificent archive is now permanently housed in Liverpool Cathedral – an appropriate home given that the building's architect was Elizabeth's uncle, Sir Giles Gilbert Scott.

In the 1980s, tastes began shifting again. With the addition of a dynamic managing director, Fiona Flint, Watts collated its archive into fabric collections. Instead of being kept as stock ranges in pattern books, they were displayed on large hangers to emphasise the scale of some of the designs and the exquisite, traditional weaving. Their names tell their own stories: Kinnersley is from a nineteenth-century castle in Herefordshire that was home to Bodley's wife; Hengrave is named after Hengrave Hall in Suffolk, a Watts commission; and Benson is after Father Benson of the Cowley Fathers.

Italian names crop up in the collection because all three of the original partners travelled in Europe. They would draw and come back with swatches of cut velvets. These were then named after their place of origin – Genoese and Ravenna, for example. There is a stamped velvet on a roller in the archive. It is a Pugin design commissioned by Crace, and was originally made for Abney Hall in

Cheshire in 1848. Today, it is made up as a chenille. Then there is a pure silk fabric designed by Thomas Garner that dates back to 1878. It is called Gothic. Hermitage is a Bodley design from the late 1880s. A large-scale symmetrical design with a floral flow, it shows the first leanings toward Art Nouveau.

BIGGER AND BETTER

The cramped confines of Tufton Street meant that other premises were needed to house the fabric and wallpaper collections. Watts & Co., the church furnishers, stayed at Tufton Street and the newly formed Watts of Westminster moved the stock, despatch and accounts to Herefordshire in 1987. In 1995, the showroom moved to Chelsea Harbour and in 1999 Watts bought Belinda Cootes Tapestries to fill the middle market. This move has proved very successful.

There are plenty of possibilities left in the Watts & Co. archive; new designs are temptingly added to the collection at regular intervals. Meanwhile, fashion trends have moved steadily in the company's direction. Having turned away from minimalism, Watts' high-end customers now want richer colours and textures, and are unafraid of large scales. Clearly, the very best quality textiles and wallpapers, made using traditional skills, have a lasting appeal that transcends fashion. **PB**

Opposite: The dramatic colour and design of this fabric is old gold/gold Veronese in a cotton chenille.

Top: Flame, a silk/cotton design in red/gold works equally well in a traditional or contemporary setting.

Above: 'Carnival' – a woven brocatelle.

TARTANS & TWEEDS

THE ISLE MILL

As long ago as the tenth century, an early form of kilt was worn in Argyllshire and the Scottish islands. By the end of the eighteenth century, it was possible to acquire kilts that were already pleated. These were fashioned in several different tartans, and were used as a means of identification for about 100 clans. The initial specifications for the tartans were very loosely worded. This has resulted in different interpretations of tartan colours from one weaver to the next, so there are now approximately 2000 registered tartans. There are also a number of Irish tartans that have been produced for each county. Tipperary, Limerick and Donegal all have their own designs, and there is also an Irish national tartan. As you can well imagine, these are particularly popular with American visitors.

The Isle Mill is run by Blair Macnaughton, and has a long tradition of weaving tartans, tweeds and wool materials for garments. These tartans, textured fabrics, paisleys, stripes and plains look stylish on chairs, sofas, curtains and walls, and help to create a cosy look in a room. The Isle Mill currently has seven pattern books of coordinating fabric ranges, with names like Strathtay and Lochwinnock.

The business was established by one of Blair Macnaughton's ancestors in 1783. He began by spinning and weaving wool for local farmers in Aberfeldy, and soon had a small business. At the time, Aberfeldy had a rural farming community, but there was never any crofting in Perthshire. However, Perthshire did have a weaving tradition. There were jute and linen mills, and an original Cartwright wheel still exists on the River Tay.

SINCERITY AND SUCCESS

In 1835, two brothers moved to Pitlochry in Perthshire and started a spinning and weaving mill, together with a retail business, called A. & J. Macnaughton. The business was passed from father to son, but was not automatically handed down to the eldest son. Instead, the company was inherited by sons who were passionate about the business, which is thought to be one of the main reasons for its continued success.

This business is now in its seventh generation, but was very nearly destroyed by fire in 1933. Eventually, the factory was rebuilt and, when war broke out, Macnaughtons turned its attention to making uniforms and blankets. After the

Above: An antique wing chair covered in Isle Mill's Navy Lewis tartan.

Opposite: Isle Mill have a range of coordinating trimmings to match their tartan ranges.

Band below: The most popular tartan – Flower of Scotland.

Above: The continuous weave Dobcross shuttle loom weaves without a selvedge for kilts.

Inset: Designs for Paisley print fabrics, which are always in fashion.

war, Blair's father (also called Blair) studied textiles in Galashiels and took over the business after his father died. It was actually easier to rebuild the business in the rural highlands of Perthshire than in the mill towns of Yorkshire, as the company was never bound to the constraints of bulk production. Tourism also helped the regeneration of the business, as Pitlochry was very popular as a post-war, spa-style resort.

Apart from wool weaving, the warehouse and the shop, the company also provided a bespoke design service. Estate workers would bring in fleece to be converted into

tweed, or a family would request a short run of their specific tartan. The company made travel rugs and blankets, as well as tweed jacket materials and plain-coloured fabrics. Fabrics were generally produced in a style known as Heather Mixture (where four or five colours are blended together). A type of Harris Tweed was also spun, sent to the Western Isles to be handled and then returned to the mill for finishing. The raw materials for the products consisted almost entirely of pure Scottish wool. Isle Mill was able to dye the wool in a large number of colours, but tried to keep the palette to a minimum. Blair has vivid childhood memories of watching dye being poured into the burn at the mill.

In 1965, A. & J. Macnaughton won the Throckmorton Challenge. This competition began in 1811 and invited weavers to see how quickly they could produce a coat made from wool that had been on a sheep's back at sunrise. Macnaughtons broke the record, and still hold it, with a time of 6 hours and 10 minutes. The fulfilment of this challenge requires a range of diverse skills, such as shearing the sheep, scouring the wool, dyeing it, carding it (teasing out the wool and combing it), spinning, warping, weaving and, ultimately, finishing.

DIVERSITY AND EXPANSION

As the town of Pitlochry began to cater for tourism, it moved away from its manufacturing base, which caused a shortage of labour. Blair's father decided to diversify by purchasing a company called House of Edgar in Edinburgh. This business was involved in the wholesale of worsted woollen fabrics.

The Macnaughtons also purchased Isle Mill, which was an estate company owned by the Keswick family. This business relocated to Aberdeen, an area of severe unemployment until oil was discovered, and mostly made tartans for kilts sold through House of Edgar.

In 1980, Blair went to Australia to be a textile designer at John Fosters (now Foster Valley), a subsidiary of a Yorkshire mill. He soon became general manager, and restructured the company in the face of the shrinking Australian textile industry. He was then headhunted by a soft furnishings company that sold fabrics to the domestic interiors and contract markets. When Blair finally returned to Scotland, he undertook a strategic review of the Mcnaughton company, and decided that it was time to expand into the domestic interiors market.

The Isle Mill supplies an extensive range of fabrics for interiors, not all of which are tartans and tweeds. There is a range called Erskine, which has eight colourways of plaids, plains, stripes and checks, as well as a cashmere range and a book of silks woven in India.

INFLUENCES FROM ABROAD

Another distinctly Scottish fabric that has been extensively used in interior design is Paisley. Paisley was originally a Kashmiri design, and first came to Scotland in the early 1800s. The design was developed in the town of Paisley in Renfrewshire, just outside Glasgow. In a similar process to that used to create Harris Tweed, the yarns were dyed and warped, then given to hand weavers in their houses. These workers were paid according to how many

Left: Many books in the Isle Mill archive show original watercolours which could be used for designs.

Tartan for a bespoke kilt order has to be measured to the knee, cut and marked for pleats

threads per inch they had to weave. By the mid-nineteenth century, the Paisley shawl was the ultimate fashion accessory. Isle Mill's book of Paisleys is called Lochwinnoch, and the company also makes throws in a number of colourways.

Men's suiting materials also work well as interior fabrics, and can add definition to the walls of a study. Particularly effective patterns include dogtooth check and plaid, as well as striped or plain wool in muted colours or tweedy textures.

Isle Mill has an archive of original hand-coloured pictures and designs, which it frequently uses as a reference base, but the company also relies on computer-aided design for its Dobby and Jacquard looms. Designing on a computer is much more flexible than by hand, and allows the option of playing around with patterning, different yarns and colours. For instance, the Lomond collection was specifically designed to introduce more colourways.

New plaids are normally restricted to six colours, because of the limitations of the machinery. However, the Jacquards can handle large pattern repeats and novelty designs. One such design is of the Scottish emblem of a lion rampant, with two sizes of repeat on a self-coloured background in a variety of colour ways, from navy blue or emerald green to heather and earthy brown. These colours can also be printed as a thistle repeat, shamrocks on emerald for Ireland and dragons for Wales, to be used as chair coverings, curtains or kilts. A range of trimmings has also been added to the Isle Mill collection, and designs are supplied to fabric wholesalers around the world.

Dyed yarns are transported on large cones to Isle Mill's factory in Keith, near Aberdeen, where they are broken down into the right quantities for each pattern. The cones are put on warping machines, which run in sections for the total width of fabric required. The warp goes on to a beam (large spindle) and is tied to the loom at the same time as the weft yarn pirns are prepared for the shuttles.

Although many of the fabrics are manufactured on high-speed rapier Jacquard looms (the Paisleys, fancy weaves and new cards from the design studio in Perth, for example), the tartans are made on continuous weave, Dobcross shuttle looms. These machines date back to 1936, and were made by Hollingsworth & Knowles. The continuous weave has no selvedge, thereby providing a clean bottom edge for kilts.

The tartan fabric process is labour intensive and therefore expensive. When the newly woven fabrics leave the looms, they are hand-checked for faults. Flaws are immediately mended. The fabric is then folded and sent to a finishing plant to be washed and wound onto rolls, in preparation for cut-length orders.

THE PRESERVATION OF TRADITION

Tartans that are destined to become kilts are shipped to Paisley, where a highly skilled workforce carries out most of the production process by hand. A bespoke kilt order, which can be heavy, medium or lightweight, has to be measured to the middle of the knee, where the tartan is cut and marked for pleats. The kilt is then tacked for pleating on chalk lines to ensure accuracy, stitched to hip length and tacked at the hem. Finally, the pleats are pressed into position.

The rules and traditions of kilt-wearing are complex and steeped in family traditions. Some clans have more than one tartan, such as dress tartan, muted (for black tie), ancient and modern for different occasions. The flashes for traditional socks are also made in the Mcnaughton's Paisley factory. These are sometimes made to match the kilt, though pipe bands usually sport a plain flash and

certain clans have no flashes at all. The plaid, which is worn diagonally from the shoulder, is for country dancing and traditional family occasions. They often feature fringe-edging or rosettes. Ties are never tartan, but are usually black or tweed. The sporran can be made from any natural source, including porcupine, beaver or white sealskin.

Approximately 50 per cent of Isle Mill's output is for the American and European markets, and of all the tartans, the most popular is the Flower of Scotland. It was made as a tribute to the late Roy Williamson, writer of the words and music to 'Flower of Scotland', which has been adopted as Scotland's alternative national anthem. It is based on the Gunn tartan, which the writer wore. Isle Mill launched this tartan in 1991 and it has since become one of the world's most recognisable patterns. Other popular tartans for interiors include Black Watch, Lindsay and, of course, a very stylish tartan called: Macnaughton. **PB**

Above: Tartan being made into a kilt. This woollen fabric is equally suitable for interior use.

Left: The correct number of spools are assembled to make a tartan fabric.

CARPETS
BRINTONS LTD.

Brintons is the largest carpet manufacturing company in Britain. It has been a Royal Warrant holder since 1957, and is a licensed partner of the National Trust. The company also won The Queen's Award for Export Achievement in 1998.

With a workforce of 2000, Brintons has an international reputation for high-quality installations, and is well-equipped to deliver large orders. It produced 35 acres of specially woven carpet for Chek Lap Kok Airport in Hong Kong, in association with the architects, Foster Associates. This carpet had to be capable of withstanding the footfall of 35 million passengers each year. The company has also supplied carpets for casinos and hotels in Las Vegas, including the MGM, The Desert Inn and The Venetian. Passengers on cruise liners, such as P&O's *Oriana* and Cunard's *QE2* and *QM2*, walk on Brintons carpets. Although hotels and public houses place the majority of the orders for high-quality, woven Axminsters, one-third of the company's business derives from the domestic market.

A HIVE OF INDUSTRY
The story behind Brintons is interwoven with the history of the Worcestershire mill town of Kidderminster. This town had the ideal

Opposite: Brintons' Abbotsford – a bold tartan carpet range for a country look in 'Macinnes' design.

Left: The first Brintons factory at Hill Pool, Chaddersley Corbett near Kidderminster.

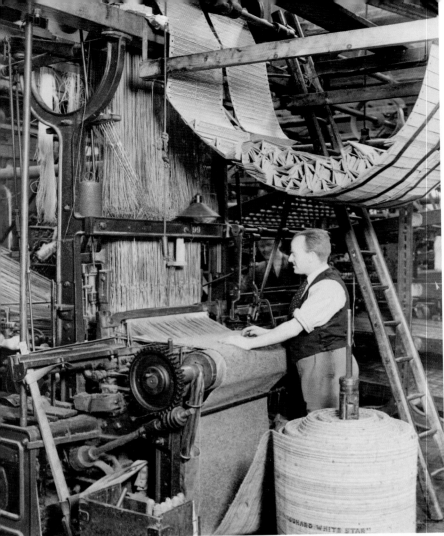

Above left: Super Wilton carpet for Cunard White Star Line's 'Queen Mary' 1935.

Above right: Brintons' shire horses transporting 36 tonnes of carpet, including the first consignment of an order for R.H. Macy & Co. Inc., New York, the largest department store in the world. This picture depicts the first stage of the journey in 1923.

Above, bottom right: The 'Bull' signals the end of the working day; Brintons in the 1940s.

Opposite: Mandarin stripe runner from the pure living range.

Opposite, inset: Tibetan Gold carpet from the Rennaissance Classics range inspired by the finest historical traditions.

conditions for weaving: sheep, a work-force and water (sourced from the River Stour) for dyeing and spinning. These natural advantages (coupled with the Staffordshire and Worcestershire canal system, a midland location and a railway network) added to the importance of Kidderminster's position as a thriving industrial centre for carpet weaving.

In 1783, William Brinton founded his company at a yarn spinning mill called Hill Pool The company also owned a dyeing and weaving factory in Mill Street. That year, 300 weavers of wool, silk and linen products were registered in the town of Kidderminster, rising to 1000 by 1807. Weaving was carried out as a cottage industry on handlooms in individual homes. The weavers produced a variety of cloths. However, the most popular fabric was known as Kidderminster 'stuff' – a heavy wool based on multi-purpose cloth, which could be placed on top of flagstone or wood floors. This was a forerunner of

the first flat carpet to be made from woollen yarn – Kidderminster.

Although knotted carpets had been made since 1000 BC in Central Asia, it was not until the eighth century that the skill was brought to Europe by Spanish Moors. By the fifteenth century, the production of knotted carpets had begun in Tournai, and by the sixteenth century the technique had spread to Antwerp. Belgian Calvinist weavers then dispersed to Ireland and England, where their work was known as 'Turkey-work'. These carpet designs were initially based on Islamic patterns.

By the early seventeenth century, knotted or Turkey-work carpet production was prolific in Europe, with Huguenot weavers producing fine examples of the craft. From 1608 to 1825, exquisite Savonnerie carpets were made in Paris. Production was then transferred to the Gobelin factory in Beauvais just north of the city. A flat tapestry carpet was produced at Aubusson,

The pure living range is easy to
coordinate throughout the home

Though a pile carpet, 'tapestry' is quicker to weave because the yarn is pre-printed

Left: Brintons' Duet in
'coconut' colourway – a
plain tufted twist carpet.

Below: Earth quartz and
network rug from the
pure living range.

a town in the Creuse area of France, renowned for pure water and bright dyes. This prosperous era came to an end in 1685, when skilled Huguenot weavers were expelled from the country under the Revocation of the Edict of Nantes. These workers were welcomed in England, where their artistic flair and consummate skill permeated the British carpet industry.

THE INDUSTRIAL REVOLUTION

Brussels carpet (a loop pile, woven on a foundation of cotton or linen with a worsted yarn) was first introduced to Kidderminster in 1749 by a weaver called John Broom. It was so popular that it outstripped all other carpet production.

The first raised-pile production of Brussels weave was a complex process. It was crafted on handlooms, and incorporated up to five colours in the pattern, so the weaver had to have an assistant. Apprenticeships were offered to children as young as ten, who were called 'draw-boys' or 'draw-girls'. The introduction of the tall Jacquard looms in 1825 meant that it was no longer practical for weavers to work from home, and loom shops became increasingly popular. These practical buildings housed between four and 16 looms.

In 1819, Henry Brinton established a carpet-weaving factory near Kidderminster town centre, and by the following year, the town's population had increased to include 2000 weavers. However, the rapid growth of this industry was soon struck down by an era of industrial disputes. The resulting poverty, together with poor sanitation and water supplies, brought on an outbreak of the Black Death.

Following this disastrous period, two new weaving processes were developed. 'Tapestry' was invented in Edinburgh by the weaver Richard Whytock. It was a pile carpet, but was quicker to weave because the yarn was pre-printed and the weavers did not need to use complicated creels of bobbins or Jacquards. The carpet could be woven as Tapestry Velvet (cut pile) or Tapestry Brussels (loop pile). Meanwhile, in Glasgow, James Templeton and William Quiglay created a patterned carpet. The finished product was called 'Chenille Axminster'.

THE GREAT EXHIBITION

Over the years, Brintons grew steadily but the Kidderminster carpet-making tradition was changed forever. In 1851, Queen Victoria's Great Exhibition was held in Joseph Paxton's Crystal Palace in Hyde Park, London. The Royal Society of Arts conceived the idea for the exhibition, with Prince Albert as President and Henry Cole as a key organiser.

The exhibition was intended to be a showcase for the 'Works Of All Nations', but was also an attempt to raise the design standards of manufactured goods. John Brinton chaired the exhibition's carpets committee, and also organised several stands to represent the crafts of Kidderminster.

Above: The Classic Florals range, traditional but in soft pretty colours. 'Tapestry aubusson' broadloom, 'tapestry jardin' broadloom and 'olive tapestry' runner.

The American power looms soon proved much more efficient to use

An American called Erastus Bigelow was also present at the exhibition, showcasing his power carpet-weaving loom. This technology involved steam engines, line-shafting and belt drives, but held no interest for Brintons and its rival Kidderminster companies. They were suspicious of the new machine, and since their businesses were thriving, they decided to stick with their existing looms. However, the Halifax carpet company John Crossley & Sons snapped up the production licences for the patented machines and soon proved that the power loom was quicker and much more efficient to use.

Eventually, having lost business to their competitors, the Kidderminster companies embraced the power loom, and adapted their businesses accordingly. In the mid-1850s, Brintons built new factory buildings for their power looms. Raw materials were stored in a five-storey mill, which was completed in 1867. The

mill was shaped like a grand piano and is still known locally as the 'piano building'. Brintons' prestigious office building was built in 1876, on the borders of Exchange Street.

Soon afterwards, disaster struck when the 'piano building' was gutted by fire. John Brinton rode to the scene on horseback, where 400 men were already fighting the flames. The fire alarm bell had gone unheard, so a loud, steam-powered foghorn was installed as a replacement. In later years, the foghorn became redundant as a fire alarm, so it was used to signal the start and end of each day's work, and was nicknamed 'The Bull'.

Another major revolution in the carpeting world was taking place in New York. In 1878, Halcyon Skinner invented the Spool Axminster, a machine that could accommodate an unlimited amount of yarn colours. The narrow-width, light-weight looms were suitable for a female workforce. Women were not initially welcomed on the factory floor, but gradually gained acceptance. Multi-coloured carpets became known as 'Axminsters'. The name Axminster originates from the town in Devon, where a multi-coloured, knotted pile carpet was first produced. In 1890, Brintons took the technology further by inventing a gripper system to insert pile tufts into the carpet, and this was subsequently patented as the Gripper Axminster loom.

ECONOMIC RECOVERY

The latter part of the nineteenth century was a time of expansion and growth, but also of conflict. Problems arose due to rapid changes in working practices, job insecurity because of mechanisation and the failure of previously prosperous carpet companies. This caused an atmosphere of growing uncertainty and unemployment. Unfortunately, the advent of the mechanical age coincided with a slump in the market-place. With unemployment rife, many industrial workers migrated to the United States, Australia, New Zealand and Canada.

Above left: Majestic carpet creates an elegant background to the pastel setting of this room.

Above: The eastern style of the Marrakesh range in colourway kasbah sun.

Opposite: A woven Axeminster Broadloom carpet in sandlewood lunar.

Right: Elda spice from the paloma range.

Opposite: Paloma design in lorca olive inspired by sunbaked colours of the Mediterranean.

Below: Brintons' Vivienne Westwood carpet dress advertisement (1993)

As a direct result, when the economy finally recovered Kidderminster found itself woefully short of skilled labour.

In spite of these difficulties, Brintons went from strength to strength. To celebrate Queen Victoria's Jubilee year in 1887, John Brinton presented Brinton Park to the people of Kidderminster. In 1904, John Brinton's seventh son, Cecil, an accomplished engineer, joined the company and set up a department for loom design. This initiative was a great success, and Brintons still designs and makes its own looms to this day.

Normal business was put on hold during the First and Second World Wars, when the looms were converted to produce blankets and webbing. Munitions were also made in the factories.

The austere post-war years were actually a time of prosperity and modernisation for Brintons. The subsequent building boom demanded a variety of floor coverings. In previous decades, the fashion had been to place a carpet square on top of a wood or linoleum floor, but by the 1960s, fitted carpets were de rigueur. The company went on to open a factory in Australia, and a spinning plant in Telford, which later became the largest yarn plant in Europe.

The raw materials for the yarn, purchased at auction, usually consist of 80 per cent wool and 20 per cent nylon. Wool from Scottish sheep that are accustomed to living on rugged terrain is ideal for carpet weaving. Wool from New Zealand is more suited to pale, clean colours. (Wool from Australian sheep is far too soft for carpet making.) Brintons opened offices in Germany and the United States, and in 1998 the company acquired US Axminster Inc. of Greenville, Mississippi. New factories were built in Portugal and India in 1990 and 1998 respectively. Back in Kidderminster, purpose-built factories sprang up on the outskirts of the town.

THE MODERN MARKET

There has always been a specialist in-house department for carpet design at Brintons. The designers have to produce innovative seasonal ranges, but also have to be well-versed in the processes and limitations of carpet making. Along with these restrictions, customer tastes have to be kept in mind, as well as popular market trends. In recent years, computer-aided design has been used to create patterns, but Brintons also has an immense archive to draw upon.

The current team of young designers specialises in both traditional and contemporary styles. Custom-made carpets and rugs can be made within eight to ten weeks. The colour palette is infinite, but 480 colours are generally used. The majority of the stock design ranges, such as Majestic, Finepoint, Bell Twist, Duet and Elegance, can be delivered within a week.

Today, Brintons is chaired by Michael Brinton, a member of the sixth generation of the family. Michael was responsible for the inspired advertising campaign wherein fashion models wore Brintons carpets as garments. Anthony Price designed one of these advertisements, which was then photographed by Patrick Lichfield. A stylish yellow floral motif carpet 'dress', designed by Vivienne Westwood and photographed by David Bailey, was spotted by Hillary Clinton, who went on to order the carpet for the yellow drawing room in the White House.

This successful family business maintains a high-quality product, using traditional skills, but is also able to predict forthcoming trends to inspire the next generation of customers. **PB**

Hillary Clinton spotted the stylish yellow floral motif carpet 'dress' and placed an order for the White House

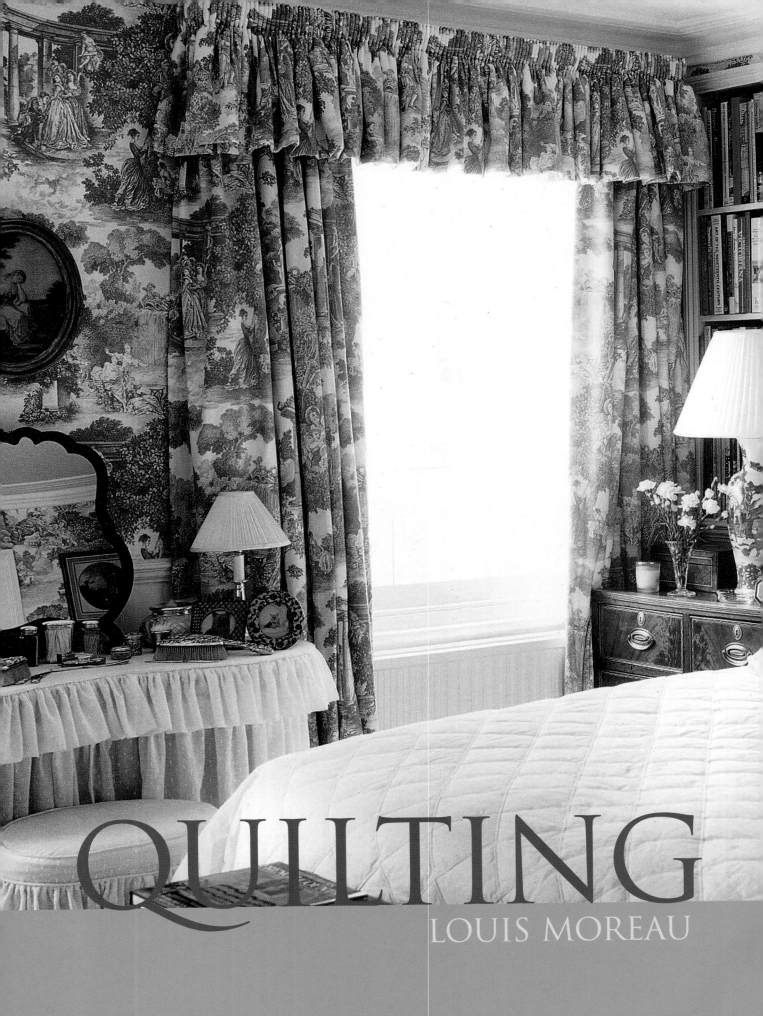

QUILTING

LOUIS MOREAU

Bed covers that have been professionally quilted add a delightful finishing touch to a bedroom. When made well, they have a long lifespan, never look creased and exude pure elegance.

Louis Moreau (The Quilters) Ltd is an exclusive, top-end quilting company that has been operating in Tottenham, North London since 1933. Its founder, Louis Moreau, was a member of The Association of Master Upholsterers and Soft Furnishers and son of Frenchman Henri Emile (known as Harry). Harry arrived in England in the early years of the twentieth century and promptly set up an embroidery business. It was there that his enterprising son learned his trade, before starting a quilting business.

The company built up a reputation for top-quality, traditional products and, from its earliest days, has produced bed coverings for the Royal Family. Back in 1934, it was commissioned to make a bedspread for the Duke and Duchess of Kent (George and Marina) that carried the owners' monograms. Then, in 1948, Louis Moreau made a quilted bedspread for the Royal baby, Prince Charles.

Thanks to the superb skills and dedication of the workforce, and the unparalleled quality control, Louis Moreau has gone from strength to strength. All of its business is trade. As well as bed covers, the company makes quilting for pelmets, upholstery, cots and cushions. Occasionally, it receives commissions for theatres and the apparel market. Embroidery for monogrammed letters is also undertaken. Customers range from interior decorators and professional curtain-making firms, to

Above top: Large square quilting for this large, perfectly proportioned bedroom.

Above: Square-shaped quilting, made with extra length to fold under the pillows.

upholsterers and quality hotels. Some ask for quilting only, others a full lining and making-up service.

Everything is done by hand. Basic training lasts at least six months and begins with the slow process of hand stitching. It takes two years to train for a variety of skills, including following a pattern. Good hand-to-eye coordination skills are essential. Training is mainly carried out by the experienced Dawn Howard, a long-serving member of staff.

The workforce is often at the mercy of the old and temperamental machines. Some are 60 years old and do not work well with certain types of fabric. It is also a problem getting them repaired. With a core staff of nine, it is advantageous if each employee can acquire more than one skill so that they can assist colleagues during busy times. Employees are from a diverse cross section of backgrounds and work together to achieve a high standard of work. Younger people are actively encouraged to join the business.

The woman responsible for running Louis Moreau is Victoria Rutter, an enterprising former fashion design student who knows every aspect of this precise business and can turn her hand to a variety of technical skills. Previously, Victoria worked in retail fashion fabrics at Dickins & Jones, supervising and managing the department. She then moved on to Liberty, where she ran the

Preparation has to be very precise to produce a professional finish

silk department. Her skills developed further through work for an interior design company, where she was in charge of quoting and ensuring that items were delivered on time. This experience has proven invaluable in her role at Louis Moreau.

SELECTING A STITCH

The process of quilting has not changed over the years. French Cornely machines introduced by the company's founder, Louis Moreau, produce the chain stitch, while a German Pfaff machine with double needles is used for raised Italian quilting (pin tuck). There is also a lock stitch machine for plain stitch work. All require the machinist to hand-guide the quilting.

First, the fabric and the wadding (which come from the West Midlands in varying weights) are tacked together at regular intervals. For diamond quilting, the fabric is prepared diagonally to the centre and then turned and repeated from all four corners. In all cases, preparation has to be very precise to produce a professional finish.

Unless the client has expressed a preference, Victoria will often decide which type of quilting should be used for a particular fabric. For instance, she thinks that raised Italian double stitch looks good on a plain background, but is lost on a strong pattern. Outline quilting looks superb on a large pattern or where a floral design can be picked out. Lock stitch can be used in channels (good for stripes), squares (for checks) or diamonds (excellent on plain fabric). Victoria herself has made a series of templates for rounded corners, scalloped edges, wavy channels and onion waves.

Budget can be a deciding factor in the selection of a quilting style. Naturally, the more complicated and individual the work, the more expensive it is.

Victoria is very aware of fashion trends. Backed by her highly skilled team, she is planning to develop exclusive new ranges under the Louis Moreau label. These will include bed covers with soft furnishing accessories that will be sold in exclusive retail outlets. **PB**

Below left: A template for scalloped edges.

Below right: Fabric is pinned to the size of the square or diamond shape before stitching.

Bottom: A quilt is expertly guided into the sewing machine.

LEATHER
J. CRISP

Opposite: Detail of an inlaid leather desktop showing the gold tooling edges.

Left: Delivering a Sedan chair in the early 1960s.

There has been a major leather-working centre in Bermondsey, South London, since 1392. In 1703, it was granted a Royal Charter by Queen Anne. During Victorian times, workers in rawhide aprons and gaiters (famously described by Charles Dickens) would take piles of skins to the local leather market to sell. Today, the industry has all but disappeared from the area, but the street names still bear testament to its history: Leather Market, Leather Market Street, Tanner Street, Morocco Street and so on.

Joseph Crisp started his leather business in Bermondsey about 200 years ago. Now in its fifth generation, the family-run company has gradually been forced northwards – from Seven Dials to Tottenham Court Road, and from Camden Town to its present address in Highgate, North London. It is here that the current Mr Crisp (the

Natural leather cowhide looks like thick white paper and has to be hand-polished

fifth Joseph) conducts his business of creating leather-inlaid desk and table-tops, book spines, antique restoration, and other related crafts.

TABLES, CHAIRS AND BOOKS

There were once many small tanneries scattered throughout the UK, but only three remain (two in Scotland and one in Kent). It is from these sources that Joseph Crisp obtains his finished, ready-dyed hides and more exclusive natural hides. Natural hides are used for hand dyeing, a complex process that requires a great deal of skill.

Natural leather cowhide looks like thick white paper and has to be hand polished, sealed and then carefully coloured by hand. Spreading the tint evenly is essential. Not all hides are the same, so the skill is in matching them. Leather can also fade over time, especially if it has been exposed to strong sunlight. A customer of Percy Bass, for example, may have a set of six matching antique, leather dining room chairs and require an additional two to enlarge the set. Crisp's skilled cabinet makers will first reproduce the frame and then find identical, traditional upholstery.

At present, Joseph Crisp is working on a Pugin carved oak armchair (c.1840). Many similar pieces have been through the workshop over the years, but are becoming more rare. Crisp suspects that this particular chair came from a deconsecrated church, which would probably have had a room with several chairs for meetings and wedding registrations. Badly restored some 20 years ago, the chair is now being returned to its original form – without springs or rubber filling. The only modern item Joseph may use, with permission from the owner, is staples. The antique industry used to despise staples, but seems to be taking a softer stance because they are much kinder to wood than tacks.

Joseph Crisp's speciality is leather inlay for desks and tables, which is a large part of the business. Depending on the budget, he makes the inlay from either ready-dyed or hand-coloured natural leather. A higher grade of leather must be used for furniture, as it cannot be too soft or stretchy. After he has attached the leather to the furniture, Joseph sends the piece to the Crisp factory where it is tooled. If it is a lovely antique bureau with ormulu mounts and brass inlay, for example, a large central motif and extravagant designs in all four corners would be perfect. However, most requests tend to be for less elaborate gold edging.

Below left: A chair in the workshop awaiting restoration.

Below right: The finished leather button back chair.

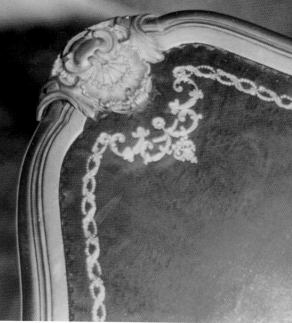

Prior to the 1800s, edging was with gold leaf and a very slow process. Now it is carried out using gold foil on a roll, with the choice of roller determining the pattern. Two employees at Crisp's specialise in this skilled work and continue to use the 200-year-old rollers that the business has owned since its inception. A gas ring heats the roller to exactly the right temperature – too cool and the glue on the back of the tape will not melt, too hot and it will burn the hide.

Book spines are popular for concealing all manner of appliances – fridges, televisions, video and DVD players, and safes, to name a few. But they are troublesome and expensive to make. Indeed, a row of spines can cost far more than a set of old, leather-bound books. Crisp personally believes that quality resin reproductions are perfectly acceptable, but will never turn a job away.

MOVING WITH THE TIMES

In-house work aside, Crisp's can supply leather desktop inlays for export. Its one provision is that it receives very accurate measurements. The company will also supply leather to Percy Bass for upholstery. In fact, trade flows both ways because Crisp's will sometimes require the knowledge and expertise of Jane Morris – particularly when a job involves re-upholstering.

Leather is not the only material Joseph handles. Recently, he has been asked to work with Alcantara, a synthetic suede fabric that has the advantage of added width. So while this is an old, established company with a proud history, Joseph Crisp's is still evolving. Its owner has made one notable detour from family tradition, however – not one of his three sons is called Joseph. **PB**

Above top: Lea and Mick, the leather gilders at the workshop in Chalk Farm, late 1970s. The gilding irons hang on the walls.

Above left: A selection of gilding irons in the Crisp workshop.

Above right: Gold tooling follows the curved lines on the corner of this French desk.

40

PLEATING

F. CIMENT

During the Regency period, it was very fashionable to have pleated fabric fitted behind wire or brass grille cabinet doors. In those days, the pleating of the silk or moiré would have been done by hand. Later, during the years 1860–70, machines were invented that could quickly produce different types of pleating.

The pleating used in today's interiors has much the same purpose as the original examples; it lines mesh-fronted cabinets or wardrobes that have either glass or chicken-wire panelled fronts. Various styles of pleating are also used to border the leading edge of curtains, edge fabric tiebacks and festoon blinds.

F. Ciment was established in the 1920s or 1930s by an elderly lady who pleated for designers such as Christian Dior, Hardy Amies and Norman Hartnell. It was soon amalgamated with another firm called West End Pleating, run by Frank Weinert. Weinert mostly dealt with bulk-order business for companies like Fred Perry. About 30 years ago, his sons Terry and Leslie took over. Today, it is Terry who runs the business.

Until 1990, the Ciment factory operated just off Oxford Street. Up to that time the streets surrounding this major shopping street were buzzing with small factories that were engaged in the garment trade. Everything was nearby – zips, fabrics, buttons, ribbons. A change in planning regulations forced these small industries out of the area and Ciment subsequently moved to Walthamstow, and then to its present location in Harold Wood, Essex.

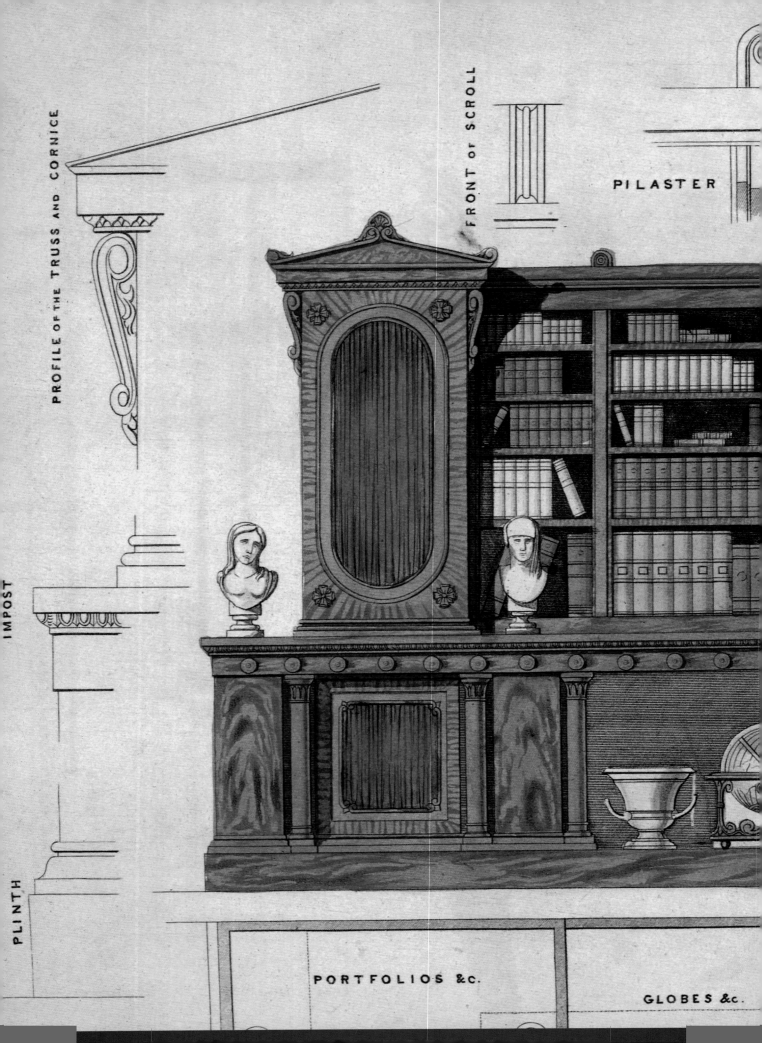

PROFILE OF THE TRUSS AND CORNICE

FRONT OF SCROLL

PILASTER

IMPOST

PLINTH

PORTFOLIOS &c.

GLOBES &c.

A FASHIONABLE BUSINESS

At F. Ciment, each new design needs a new template. Brown card is marked with pinpricks, folded and steamed into place. Fabric is then placed between two rolls of paper before being fed into one of four machines (each for a different type of pleat) that date from the 1920s. Card templates are kept for as long as possible because it can take up to 80 hours to make replacements for the most complicated ones. In fact, probably only a handful of people in the country know the very complicated origami folding techniques needed to create intricate pleating patterns such as chevrons, basketweave, pinetree, opal and others.

The types of pleating most commonly used for interiors are flat, straight pleats. Widths depend on the customer's request and on the natural repeat of the fabric. Accordion pleats and box pleats are also popular, and there is a big demand for pleated headboards for hotel rooms. Since there is only a 10 per cent demand for this specialist skill in the decorating trade, most of F. Ciment's business is, and always has been, in fashion. The oldest known garment in existence, which was made about 4000 years ago, is pleated.

Over the years, pleating has been incorporated into garments for a variety of eminent clients, including HM Queen Elizabeth II and the Princess of Wales. Ciment pleated the dress The Queen wore to the wedding of Prince Charles and Lady Diana Spencer, and Terry Taylor (Terry Weinert's assistant) once worked for Nettie Vogues, a couture house in W1 that has designed dresses for, among

Flat, straight pleating is the type most commonly used for interiors

others, Princess Diana. The designers of the future often spend half a day at the Ciment factory to learn how pleating is done. Ex-students include Mary Quant and Zandra Rhodes.

Theatrical costumes are another area of the Ciment business, with recent commissions including 'The Lion King', 'Phantom of the Opera', 'Les Miserables' and the Norwegian Opera. The company's most high-profile costume of all, however, was the Bolero outfit for ice-skating stars Torvill and Dean. Terry worked closely with designer Courtney Jones to perfect the purple sleeves that became part of those iconic performances in Sarajevo and Ottawa in 1984. **PB**

Opposite: A bookcase design published by George Smith in 1826 showing pleated fabric door panels.

Below: The pleated card and iron weights used to make pleated fabrics.

CURTAIN POLES

MCKINNEY & CO.

P ercy Bass relies on several 'support' services. One of these, an innovative business selling antique curtain poles and finials, started out in 1987 on the rear ground floor of the Percy Bass premises. At the time, the company was known as McKinney Kidston. It was run by Shona McKinney, who had a business background, and Kath Kidston, an interior decorator. Kath later decided to set up shop on her own, leaving Shona to take the company forward with her custom-made finial designs.

Opposite: An abundance of choice in the McKinney showroom includes pelmets, coronas, finials, door handles and curtain poles.

Above: A rosette and lion head – just two of the mofits available from a large selection.

The business grew organically and demand for the finials exceeded supply. Although it was much easier to source antique curtain fittings in the 1980s than it is now, many customers placed orders that were simply too large to fulfil. This encouraged the production of good-quality replicas. In fact, the quality was so good that it was virtually impossible to tell the difference between old and new.

By 1990, the business had outgrown the Percy Bass rooms and moved to larger premises on Wandon Road, off New King's Road in Chelsea. It then moved again to Battersea. Items assembled there include bespoke curtain poles, finials, bedposts, doorknobs and handles. They have a variety of finishes – from wood, brass and nickel to glass, acrylic and, more recently, leather and snakeskin. McKinney & Co.

Above and below: Imaginative finials for curtain poles, and innovative door and cupboard handles.

Opposite: Pondicherry curtain fabric by Bennison is teamed with a McKinney & Co. wood curtain pole colour-matched with the David Linley bookcase. The wing chair is covered in a Claremont silk/linen, with the cushion covered in Bennison's Toile Clemenceau I Gris Bleu.

uses several subcontractors – metal workers, woodworkers and leather, Perspex and glass specialists – to manufacture pieces from Shona's original ideas.

Shona is very creative and is always thinking of original ways to take her products forward artistically. However, she does not draw her ideas herself. When an artist completes the drawings and the samples have been made and approved to Shona's exacting standards, they are added to the catalogue. All the finials have 'F' numbers and currently range from F1 to F174, which is a huge choice. Finishes come in all combinations, and wood can be stained to any colour to match customers' existing furniture.

For the most part, the company uses poplar wood for its poles, bedposts and accessories. It is a good, hard wood without knots and takes easily to staining. Shona never uses mahogany for environmental reasons. The newest of these items have leather finials with inserted leather leaves and an underside covered in snakeskin.

Following the success of its poles, finials and bedposts, McKinney & Co. branched out into pelmets and coronas. Wooden pelmets can either be plain or decorated with stars and rococo scrolls. Coronas can be shaped like crowns (popular for children's rooms) or made to resemble fretwork with floral motifs. The possibilities are enormous; so enormous in fact that there are very few orders that do not deviate at all from the standard catalogue.

Matching tiebacks and rosettes can be the perfect way to complete an interior design scheme. Recent innovations from McKinney & Co. include door hooks and door-knobs, escutcheon plates and newel posts. Doorknobs can be made from brass, nickel and glass in unlimited combinations. All the door hooks have concealed fixings.

Bay windows used to pose particular difficulties for curtain poles. Shona came up with two solutions, both requiring good templates. One pole has angled joins, and the other is curved (made with great difficulty). The latter is joined at the back with a neat dovetail that is not visible from the front of the pole.

McKinney & Co. uses traditional skills to create stunning accessories for the home, and takes pride in every small detail. Orders range from the classical to the wacky. Clear Perspex poles can be filled with lavender, shells or even wine corks. If a customer wants a leather-clad pole, this is made with a layer of Perspex so that the rings can glide along it easily. The beech rings can be covered in leather, too.

In short, McKinney & Co. is a customer-led business that offers a high-quality, bespoke service. Any item can be delivered within three to four weeks of ordering. **PB**

TEXTILE BLOCK PRINTING
EDWARD TURNBULL

Turnbull's is the last company in the world to make hand-blocked furnishing fabrics. For this reason, the company, situated just outside Manchester, is considered a treasure by those in the interior decorating trade.

Edward Turnbull established the company in the late 1960s. However, the origins of the business go back much further to 1881, when it was called Turnbull & Stockdale. In those days, it was a vertically integrated company with various outlets, including wholesale showrooms in Manchester and London.

Turnbull & Stockdale produced its own collections in its own studios, and manufactured in its own factories. The range of printing styles on offer included hand-block, surface roller, duplex (which is printed on both sides), copper roller and screen printing.

Although it did not spin its own yarn, the company had separate factories for weaving, dyeing and bleaching, as well as

wholesale distribution and curtain-making units. Turnbull's still owns some of these premises; the bleaching shed is now used as the company headquarters and the weaving shed as a base for hand-block printing.

Though established in the late 1960s, the company has roots going back to 1881

Turnbull & Stockdale was closed down after its new owners, Reed International, rationalised some of the manufacturing at its site in Uxbridge. Realising that Reed International saw the hand-block printing unit as a liability, Edward Turnbull approached the company to see if he could acquire it. He succeeded. With the help of the printers, the block tables were moved to a factory in Ramsbottom, near Manchester. The precious hand blocks were all

Opposite: Hand-blocked printed fabric – 'Hollyhock' by Lee Jofa (reduced scale).

Left: Highly skilled craftsmen in the second stage of hand blocking.

Inset left: Hand-carved blocks.

Opposite: Screen printed fabric – Sanibel by Schumacker (reduced scale).

A variety of base cloths can be used for hand-block printing, including wool, linen, hessian, cotton and silk. The production process is incredibly labour intensive and highly skilled. Some hand blockers have been with the company for more than 40 years, and it is increasingly difficult to recruit talented apprentices.

SCREEN-PRINTING

Traditionally, North America has always been the largest market for hand-block printing, so Turnbull's initially concentrated its efforts in this area. Lee Jofa has always been a significant hand-block printing customer, along with a number of American decorators, including Fonthill and Hazeton House. However, English companies such as Warner & Son and G.P. & J. Baker, style leaders in the 1970s, also had several hand blocks in their print ranges.

transported in the back of Edward's Triumph Herald estate car. In 1968, the hand-block printing unit was re-established under the name Edward Turnbull & Co.

The Turnbull archive of hand blocks has diverse origins. Some are owned by individual fabric houses, and are stored at Turnbull's to be used when a particular design is required. Others are original Turnbull & Stockdale blocks, some dating back as far as 1860. The blocks are usually hand-carved from sycamore, with a pine base inside. Wood, felt and copper blocks are also used. As various printers ceased production, their blocks have found their way to Turnbull's, ensuring the establishment of a vast printing archive. All of the blocks require extensive maintenance, and sometimes have to be replaced.

The business has gone from strength to strength, and is now run by Edward's son, Paul Turnbull. It employs 85 people, some of whom work on a three-shift basis. Fabric companies bring their designs to Turnbull's to have them reproduced, but some customers require a different process from hand-blocking. They want to achieve the feeling and the look of a hand-worked fabric, without the expense. This led the company into the realms of another highly specialised printing process – screen-printing.

Screen-printing can
achieve the look
and feel of a
hand-worked fabric

There are very few specialist textile screen printers in the world. Turnbull's is the largest one in the UK, and there are only a handful of others in Europe. Even in this highly specialised area, Turnbull's occupies a unique niche because of the way the company has developed its hand-block printing processes to accommodate screen-printing.

When Turnbull's first started screen-printing, the process was carried out on long tables with hand screens. Every screen had to be moved along the table. The company then switched to using automated machines that lifted the screen, moved it, dropped and printed. The latest generation of machinery is highly computerised, and is based on Italian apparel printing. The screen is stationary and the blanket moves, but the printing principle is the same. Each colour has to dry before the next colour lands on top, which makes the process exceptionally exacting compared to the majority of fabric production.

Apart from having a precisely controlled printing effect, the new machines also allow the regulation of the drying environment, which is important for batch consistency. This sophisticated method of printing allows Turnbull's to reproduce the fine-line detailing and block-print looks that established its reputation.

For the most part, the colours used for hand-block printing are vat dyes. This is a method whereby the colour is activated by exposure to steam and creates a chemical affinity with the fibre. The residue is then washed off to reveal a localised area of dye. Another dyeing method, which is only occasionally used for unusual base cloths, is pigment dyeing. In this instance, a coloured, glue-like substance is put on the surface of the fabric and baked. This method is often used to print silks.

DESIGN REALISATION

Although Turnbull's was first established as a commission printers, it also offers its customers a valued support system to

A sophisticated method of printing allows Turnbull's to reproduce fine-line detailing

Opposite: Curtain fabric by Ralph Lauren. Sofa covered in Andrew Martin Molesuede and contrast piped by Brunschwig & Fils.

Left: A quirky table top arrangement of cricket balls.

Below: Cushions (left to right) are Ralph Lauren, Nicholas Haslam and Brunschwig & Fils.

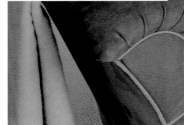

Customers like the fact that they can update some aspects of a room, while retaining others

interpret their design ideas. Turnbull's does not have a prime design department, but its experienced staff can readily make client ideas reality. Usually, fabric houses start the creative process between nine months and two years ahead of the launch of a new range. Even with the wealth of archive designs available at Turnbull's, there are only a finite number of undiscovered gems to be unearthed.

Depending on a client's wishes, Turnbull's can contribute to any aspect of design – from scale through to colouring. It also makes up samples for inspection. These are offered in repeat units on a number of base cloths. Some studios are autonomous in their design and initial colourings, and have a strong brand identity to capture the

imagination of their regular customers. These customers are attracted to the fact that they can update some aspects of a room, whilst retaining other pieces in the same colour band. One studio might produce a very loose brief, or a hand drawn picture, while another will send exact chips for every single colour. Turnbull's then interprets the artwork to provide the client with the best possible printing solution. If a client has a more specific request, Turnbull's can send a toile de Jouy to France for further attention. Computer-aided design is used extensively in the printing process, alongside hand production. In the modern world, both have their merits.

Turnbull's takes pride in seeing design ideas translated into commercial success, and

hopes that some will become the classics of the future. Care and 'polish' at the initial stages can make all the difference to how well, and for how long, a pattern sells and survives. A long life cycle is a mark of success in a society that is constantly driven by the desire for 'new' products.

Turnbull's is currently experimenting with fabric patterns for the future, including a number of floral designs. Following the dominance of plains in the marketplace, patterns seem set to resurface. Although flower motifs never disappeared, the new generation of florals are brightly coloured, with a more contemporary interpretation. These florals are ideal for customers who may not remember the original surge of chintz. In contrast to this modern movement, there is still a demand for classical designs featuring velvets and other fabrics.

Paul Turnbull is more concerned about what a product looks like than how long it takes to produce. So the company aims to maximise printing aesthetics, rather than waste time chasing the latest equipment. While most companies have moved into faster and faster methods of production, Turnbull's investment has been geared towards improving the print mark and visual appeal of its products. This ethos is underpinned by the traditional values of good design and pride in workmanship. This is why so many of the brand leaders in the fabric wholesale business turn to this Ramsbottom-based company for quality, expertise and the preservation of traditional skills. **PB**

Opposite: This drawing room has symmetrical elements in the wing chairs, the pair of mirrors, and blue and white Chinese garden seats. Other objects are offset to create interest. The room's focal point is the stunning central photograph. The coral silk taffeta curtains are by Waris Vianne, wing chairs covered in fabric by Zimmer & Rohde and cushions by Fortuny.

Above: The brown chair in the foreground is designed with fabric by Sahco Hessein, piped in Andrew Martin. The stool is covered in Colefax & Fowler's Malabar.

CHAIR
FRAME-MAKERS
H. VAUGHAN LTD.

W hen a client orders a sofa or set of chairs from Percy Bass, the scale drawings go straight to the workshop of H. Vaughan Ltd. in East London. This family firm is the only one in London that can provide specialist custom-made chair frame designs. Without its expertise, maintaining the highest quality upholstery would be an impossible task.

Herbert Vaughan started his chair frame-making company in 1902. His ancestors had a history in furniture and cabinet making, having traded in the East End since the 1830s. That area of London, specifically Shoreditch and Bethnal Green, was an established centre for furniture making. During the eighteenth century, in the days of Chippendale and Sheraton, bespoke furniture of exceptional quality would have been made for specific homes and shipped with difficulty all around the country. In the nineteenth century, the rising middle class required a different type of service. As well as one-off designs, they wanted good-quality, standardised manufactured items that were modestly priced. Production was helped by steam-driven woodworking machinery and distribution made easier by the growing railway network.

FROM EAST END TO EAST INDIA
As was customary in the late nineteenth century, Herbert and his two brothers were 'put to the workbench' as soon as they left school aged 14. It wasn't long before they got

Above: Thomas Moss, upholsterer, in his workshop at Calvert Avenue, Shoreditch, c.1906. He was Alfred Vaughan's brother-in-law.

Opposite: A traditional room with sofas by Percy Bass with Vaughan chair frames. Curtains are by Percheron with Smith & Brighty trimmings. Sofas are covered in Rubelli with Clermont and Zimmer & Rohde cushions.

tired of the life. First his brothers, then Herbert left their father's employment.

Herbert ran away to sea, but later returned to London. At the age of 21, he decided to start up as a chair maker. He acquired rental premises in Hoxton and began assembling chairs from ready-made parts, fixing the legs and rails together with his hand-made dowels (headless wooden pegs). Although his was one of many similar businesses competing for the same orders, Herbert Vaughan managed to survive and prosper. The secret, he found, was to provide customers with a specialist service.

The business progressed, no doubt helped by the fact that Vaughan's grandfather and father-in-law were both in the upholstery business. Upholsterers, not private customers, ordered the frames for individual pieces of furniture – a custom that still survives today. Eventually, Vaughan's moved to larger premises in Bethnal Green where it made 'stuff-over'

sofa and chair frames from best-quality Canadian birch. It also acquired a trade mill, which allowed it to produce Queen Anne cabinet legs and frets.

Working conditions were harsh at the workshop. The hours were long and the pay was low. There was no heating in winter and some of the machines were in an open yard with just a corrugated iron roof for protection. Horse-drawn vehicles brought the timber, and barrow boys collected and delivered the completed frames.

By the mid-1920s, 18 men were employed at Vaughan's. One of these

was Bert Vaughan who, like his father, had started at the company the day after he left school. His two brothers, Leonard and Reginald, soon joined him – as did uncle Francis, who would later found the Association of Master Upholsterers. By 1939, most of the family and workforce had offered their services to the Second World War effort and the regular orders disappeared. The business operated on a limited scale, with most of the machinery shipped out of London for safe keeping. When it suffered a direct hit by an incendiary bomb, the company was forced to cease trading.

After the war, the East End's status as a centre for woodwork came to an end. The air raids had devastated the whole area, with many workshops and subcontractors' homes having to be demolished. While manufacturers in the provinces took over some of the furniture-making market, Vaughan's set up in new premises in Brick Lane. There, it started making utility furniture frames in two simple styles.

Timber was rationed at first. When the controls were lifted, the company decided to concentrate on making quality, individually designed frames for their regular customers. Canadian birch was no longer available, so frames were made of beech (continental rather than the English variety, which tends to warp). The best types came from Yugoslavia or Romania. African sapele, which is a type of mahogany, American cherry, oak and ash were also favourites.

In 1975, the Brick Lane premises were due for demolition, so H. Vaughan Ltd. relocated to larger premises near the East India Docks. Bert retired shortly afterwards. Today, his sons Hales and James run the business. Michael and Paul, James's sons, have assured the survival of the dynasty as they too work for the company now.

A SPECIAL RELATIONSHIP

Over the years, the firm has built up a specialist trade producing one-off designs that require a high degree of craftsmanship. It has received many interesting orders, including frames for the Royal Palace in Saudi Arabia and seating for Cunard's *QE2* liner. Other commissions have been as varied as a replica set of chairs for The Guildhall (to commemorate Admiral Lord Nelson's victory of the Nile), and 1660s chairs, stool frames and a Chair of State for the Queen's House at Greenwich. In 1999, on the request of English Heritage, Vaughan's used photographs of the original rooms at Eltham Palace to make frames for replica soft furnishings.

Most of H. Vaughan's work comprises of frames for the company's loyal customers: upholsterers like Percy Bass who make quality upholstered sofas and chairs using traditional methods. Interestingly, the two businesses have been trading since the time of Mr Bass and Bert Vaughan, making for a long, profitable partnership. **PB**

Below: A perfectly proportioned classic sofa covered in fabric and bullion fringe by Colefax & Fowler. Cushions are in Eaton check.

Bottom: Quality frames made by H. Vaughan and upholstered by Candido de Silva for Percy Bass.

Opposite: A chair being assembled in the Vaughan workshop.

ACKNOWLEDGEMENTS

The author would like to thank all of the following people for their support with this book, and giving so freely their time and enthusiasm: Edward Asprey, Karen Beauchamp, Franco Bertagnin, Jane Brighty, Michael Brinton LL, Brocket Hall International Ltd., Evelyn Brooks, Michael & Linda Campbell, Nigel Carew Jones, Philip Cayford QC, Juliette Clancy, Judy Clark & Seamus, Christopher Clegg, Annie Cleland, Peter Colbourn, Toby Colbourn, Eeva Creal, Joseph Crisp, Americo Dias, Christiane Eichstaldt, Alexander Elias, Meris Erda, Ana Ericksen, Anthony Evans, Ishbel Fleming-Boyd, Fiona Flint, Caroline Garnham, David Gazeley, Nicholas George, Jeremy Goodwin, Fiona Grant, Danny Green, Elaine Hansen, Carina Hellemaa, David Hodges, Sophia Jameson, Nicholas Kaye, Francois Lavenir, Lutyens Design Associates, Blair Macnaughton, Shona McKinney, Ana Martinez, Rt Hon Theresa May MP, Renata Mamoud, Jennifer Moores, Georgina Orde, Chris O'Reilly, Simon Playle, Darren Pull, Lawrence Rich, Karen Richards, Victoria Rutter, Candido de Silva, Anna Smith, Marion Smith, Kevin Stewart, Fiona Sutcliffe, Duncan Swanston, Terry Taylor, Neil Thomas, Melvyn Thompson, Paul Turnbull, Hales & James Vaughan, Caroline de M Walker, John Watkins, Terry Weinert, John Wilson.

PERCY BASS INTERIOR DECORATORS

Annie Cleland: p60, p150 bottom; Christiana Eichstaldt: p5 top,p34 bottom, p40, p42, p46 top, p51, p53, p96, p98, p99, p114, p133, p170; Jennie Elias: cover top right, bottom left, p6, p29, p30, p31, p34 top, p35, p36,p38, p39, p41, p43, p45, p49, p56, p68, p69, p79 right, p94, p95, p110, p148, p150 top, p156, p163; Ishbel Fleming-Boyd: cover bottom right, p12, p22, p27, p37 top, p47, p52, p54, p59, p61, p86-88, p175; Sophia Jameson: p5 middle, p44 bottom left, p48, p93 left; Ana Martinez: cover top right, p2, p32, p33, p37 bottom, p44 bottom right, p50, p55, p72, p75, p78, p90, p168, p169, p171, p172.

ARCHIVE PHOTOGRAPHS

Niall Clutton: cover bottom left, p56, p150 top; Andreas von Einsiedel: cover top right, p6, p95, p148; Antoinette Eugster: p7, p18; Percy Bass Ltd: p9 bottom right, p16, p17, 20, 21, p44 top and middle, p62-66, p67 top, p76; Brocket Hall International Ltd: p23; Patrick Loobey: p10, p11, p14 top; RBK & C reference library local studies: p14 - all images except top; Annie Cleland: p60, p150 bottom; Caroline de M Walker: p71; Maecenas Ltd: p81-85, Carew Jones: p89, p91; Smith & Brighty: p92, p96 left; John Boyd Textiles: p100-03, 105; Christies Images Ltd: p104, Lutyens Design Associates: p104 inset; Cole & Son: p108; Gainsborough Silk Weaving Co: p115-118; Titchmarch & Goodwin: p120-123; Watts of Westminster: p125, 127-131; The Isle Mill: p132; Brintons Ltd: p138-147; J Crisp: p153, 154, 155 top & bottom right; RIBA Library Photographs Collection: p158; McKinney & Co: p160-162, p163 top; Edward Turnbull: p164, p167; H Vaughan Ltd: p173; – (p106-7 by Philip Cayford with kind permission from the Department of Heritage & Works of Art).

BIBLIOGRAPHY

Images Of England - Chelsea. Patrick Loobey, 1999 (Tempus)
The Times of Chelsea, October 1974
What's On In London, 14 May 1971
Chelsea Post, 1 September 1970
Chelsea Post, 16 July 1971
Chelsea News, 9 September 1966
Vogue, December 1972
Chelsea from the five fields to the World's End, Richard Edmonds, 1956 (Phene Press)
Artists Houses in London, Giles Walkley 1994 (Scolar Press)
The London Encyclopedia. Ben Weinreb & Christopher Hibbert, 1983 (Papermac)
The Fascination of London - Chelsea. G.E.Mitton, 1902 (A & C Black)
Chelsea Past, Barbara Denny, 1996 (Historical Publications)
The Cadogan Estate, Robert Pearman, 1986 (Haggerston Press)
Castle Cary, Michael McGarvie FSA, 1980 (Avalon Industries)
Inside the House of Lords, Clive Aslet & Derry Moore, 1998 (Harper Collins)
The Palace of Westminster, Sir Robert Cooke, 1987 (Burton Shira Ltd)
The Houses of Parliament, History-Art-Architecture, Christine Riding & Jacqueline Riding, 2000 (Merrell Publishing Ltd)
Pugin, Paul Atterbury & Clive Wainwright, 1994 (Victoria & Albert Museum)
A.W.N. Pugin & The Pugin Family, Alexandra Wedgwood, 1985 (Victoria & Albert Museum)
Christopher Dresser, Widar Halen, 1993 (Phaidon)
Design & The Decorative Arts, Michael Snodin & John Styles, 2001 (V & A Publications)
Authentic Décor - The Domestic Interior 1620-1920, Peter Thornton, 1984 (Weidenfeld & Nicholson)
Eighteenth Century Decoration, Charles Saumarez Smith, 1993 (Weidenfeld & Nicholson)
Victorian Style, Judith & Martin Miller, 1993 (Mitchell Beazley)
Nineteenth-Century Decoration, Charlotte Gere, 1989 (Weidenfeld & Nicholson)

A History of English Wallpapers, 1925 (The Wall Paper Manufacturer Ltd)
The Encyclopedia of Dog Breeds, Juliette Cunliffe, 1999 (Parragon)
The Penguin book of Decorative Arts, John Fleming & Hugh Honour, 1989 (Viking)
Regency Style, Steven Parissien, 1992 (Phaidon)
Ackermann's Regency Furniture & Interiors, Pauline Agius, 1984 (The Crowood Press)
The Cabinet Maker & Upholsterer's Drawing Book, Thomas Sheraton, 1972 (Dover Publications Inc NY)
The Craftsman's Handbook "Il Libro dell' Arte", Cennino d'Andrea Cennini/Daniell V. Thompson, Jr., 1960 (Dover Publications Inc. NY)
Where We Used To Work, Kenneth Hudson, 1980 (John Baker Publishing Ltd)
The Vaughans, East End Furnisher Makers, Anthony Vaughan, 1984 (Inner London Education Authority)
Pitman's Common Commodities & Industries - Carpets, R S Brinton, 1919 (Sir Isaac Pitman & Sons)
Woven in Kidderminster, Melvyn Thompson, 2002 (David Voice Associates)
An Illustrated Companion to the Decorative Arts, 1972, J-B Glomy, Edited: Harold Osborne
World Textiles, Mary Schoeser, 2003 (Thames & Hudson)
English Church Embroidery 1833-1953, Mary Schoeser, 1998 (Watts & Co.Ltd)
Victorian Architecture, Roger Dixon & Stefan Muthesius, 1978 (Thames & Hudson)
Joseph Paxton, John Anthony, 1973 (Shire Publications Ltd)
The Penguin Book of Design and Designers, Simon Jervis, 1984 (Penguin)
Architecture: Nineteenth and Twentieth Centuries, Henry-Russell Hitchcock, 1958 (Penguin)
Victorian House Style, Linda Osband, 1991 (David & Charles)
William Morris, Richard Tames, 2003 (Shire Publications Ltd.)
British Tradition & Interior Design, Claudia Piras & Bernhard Roetzel, 2000 (Konemann)